PHOBIAS
Their Nature and Control

Publication Number 721

AMERICAN LECTURE SERIES®

A Monograph in

AMERICAN LECTURES IN LIVING CHEMISTRY

Edited by

I. NEWTON KUGELMASS, M.D., Ph.D., Sc.D.
Consultant to the Departments of Health and Hospitals
New York, New York

PHOBIAS
Their Nature and Control

By

S. RACHMAN, M.A., Ph.D.
Institute of Psychiatry
University of London

CHARLES C THOMAS • PUBLISHER
Springfield • Illinois • U.S.A.

Published and Distributed Throughout the World by

CHARLES C THOMAS • PUBLISHER
BANNERSTONE HOUSE
301-327 East Lawrence Avenue, Springfield, Illinois, U.S.A.
NATCHEZ PLANTATION HOUSE
735 North Atlantic Boulevard, Fort Lauderdale, Florida, U.S.A.

Library of Congress Catalog Card Number: 68-18303

Printed in the United States of America
N-10

To Carla and Gideon

FOREWORD

Our Living Chemistry Series was conceived by Editor and Publisher to advance the newer knowledge of chemical medicine in the cause of clinical practice. The interdependence of chemistry and medicine is so great that physicians are turning to chemistry, and chemists to medicine, in order to understand the underlying basis of life processes in health and disease. Once chemical truths, proofs and convictions become sound foundations for clinical phenomena, key hybrid investigators clarify the bewildering panorama of biochemical progress for application in everyday practice, stimulation of experimental research, and extension of postgraduate instruction. Each of our monographs thus unravels the chemical mechanisms and clinical management of many diseases that have remained relatively static in the minds of medical men for three thousand years. Our new Series is charged with the *nisus élan* of chemical wisdom, supreme in choice of international authors, optimal in standards of chemical scholarship, provocative in imagination for experimental research, comprehensive in discussions of scientific medicine, and authoritative in chemical perspective of human disorders.

Dr. Rachman of London unravels the newer knowledge of human phobias in the light of experimental psychology to achieve clinical control of a perplexing problem. Fear is a defensive mechanism of survival values; unreasoning fear, a perversion of this mechanism emanating from some painful impression or some internal conflict; but phobia, a reversion to the mentality of a savage who walks all his days hedged in between totem and taboo.

Primitive organisms developed sensitive perceptive structures on the body surface to provide an awareness of their environment in order to seek food and avoid danger. The nervous system thus started in the skin, but the nerve cells soon withdrew into a more protected position, and the sympathetic nervous system which superintends many functions of organic life, retains the primitive features of the nervous system of lower animals. Its response is immediate, widespread and explosive, brought into action by fight, fright, or flight.

He has not learned the lesson of life who does not every day surmount a fear, a product of self-consciousness, not an accompaniment of consciousness. Ancient Greeks honored Phobos as a deity to provoke panic in their enemies by wearing his fear-masks on weapons. Hippocrates first recognized the nature of phobias, and Celsus applied the term to hydrophobia, but the phobic concept remained dormant until the mid-Nineteenth Century, when psychic phenomena were probed clinically and experimentally. A physiological theory of fear finally emerged from Cannon's demonstration of increased adrenomedullary secretion and trophotropic excitation, and more recently, a psychological theory for controlling fear led to the development of behavior theory, the most promising approach to the problem of phobias.

Systematic desensitization is the new development propounded by the author to reduce or eliminate fear/anxiety, the common core of most neuroses. Phobic reactions are thus regarded as maladaptive conditioned responses acquired in painful or frightening situations that can be altered or modified, as can any other learned response, without any consideration of the symbolic or unconscious components or underlying root causes. Learning theory considers neurotic symptoms as simple, learned habits. There is no neurosis underlying the symptom, but merely the symptom itself. Once you get rid of the symptom, you eliminate the neurosis. In the forest of his fears dwells the demon of ignorance. He cannot hope to exorcise his fears until he has confronted, penetrated and understood that forest of things and forces that causes him to be afraid. Once its understanding is clear, treatment is easy.

Phobic patients receive graded retraining in meeting feared situations and some desensitization in imagination while in a state of relaxation hypnosis. Psychopathology is thus viewed not in terms of emotional mislearning or overlearning but in terms of behavior which is troublesome or dangerous and must be reshaped by positive reinforcement. Behavior therapy considers the cause and correction of phobias the responsibility of the afflicted individual himself, hence little attention is given to the patient's emotions, only to his conduct. The objective naturalistic language of research psychiatrists is thus recapturing some of the great insights of traditional morality which religionists seem to have lost. A psychological revolution in the making emphasizes creative humanism rather than traditional metaphysics. Clearly, there is but one temple in the world, and that is the body of man. Nothing is holier than this high form. We touch heaven when we lay our hand on a human body. And the hand that helps is holier than the lips that pray.

Canst thou not minister to a mind diseas'd,
Pluck from the memory a rooted sorrow,
Raze out the written troubles of the brain,
And with some sweet oblivious antidote
Cleanse the stuff'd bosom of that perilous stuff
Which weighs upon the heart?

I. Newton Kugelmass, M.D., Ph.D., Sc.D., *Editor*

INTRODUCTION

Behavior therapy is a term used to describe a number of new psychotherapeutic methods which have been developing during the past few years. Although the actual therapeutic procedures vary from aversion therapy to desensitization, they share many theoretical assumptions (Rachman, 1963; Eysenck, 1960, 1964). Behavior therapy derives its impetus from experimental psychology and has been strongly influenced by the theories of Hull, Skinner, Mowrer, Wolpe and Eysenck. According to Eysenck (1963) the "main conception unifying all these different approaches has been the belief that behavioural disorders of the most divergent type are essentially *learned responses,* and that modern learning theory (in its widest sense) has much to teach us regarding the acquisition and extinction of such responses." The application of the ideas, methods and findings of experimental psychologists to clinical problems has led to significant advances in therapy and has undoubtedly improved the prognosis for phobic illnesses.

In most textbooks, phobias are discussed in a comparatively brief manner. They are usually mentioned as a minor subcategory (or feature) of anxiety states or obsessional disorders. In recent years, however, phobias have attracted considerable attention in their own right. This change can be attributed to the development of behavior therapy, which has not only produced gratifying results with phobic disorders, but has also enlivened the entire subject of human phobias.

Until the advent of behavior therapy, phobias presented a difficult therapeutic problem. Pessimistic views about the likelihood of achieving successful results with this disorder were expressed in various psychiatric texts. Henderson and Gillespie (1950), for example, state that "phobias (in children) are much more difficult to treat than the other symptoms of psychoneurotic anxiety." Curran and Partridge (1955) expressed the opinion that "phobic symptoms are notoriously resistant to treatment, and their complete removal is rarely achieved."

More recently, Errera and Coleman (1963) reported their findings in a long-term follow-up study of nineteen phobic patients who were reassessed after an average period of twenty-three years. The therapeutic results obtained in these phobic patients were very poor; eighteen of the nineteen patients were still phobic, and Errera and Coleman argue that "phobic states occurring in adult patients tend to persist over long periods of time and seem to be uninfluenced by the relatively brief psychotherapeutic procedures of a psychiatric clinic."

Other texts are very guarded, or even evasive, about the prospects of providing satisfactory treatment for phobic patients. (See, for example, Mayer-Gross, Slater and Roth, 1960; Masserman, 1955; Diethelm, 1955; Noyes and Kolb, 1958.) This older, pessimistic outlook is now being modified as a result of the favorable results which have been obtained with behavior therapy.

The most effective technique for treating phobias which has emerged from these applications so far is *systematic desensitization.* This technique, among others, was developed by Professor Wolpe over ten years ago and is now being subjected to close investigation. The nature and the current status of this method are discussed in Chapters IV and V.

One of the main assumptions underlying the use of behavior therapy is the notion that anxiety is a central feature in most neuroses. Because anxiety and fear can, for most purposes, be regarded as similar phenomena, behavior therapists have concentrated on developing methods which reduce or eliminate fear/anxiety. Furthermore, as phobias may be regarded as persistent, excessive fear reactions, it is not surprising that behavior therapists have had to examine the nature of this particular disorder in some detail.

During the past five years a new theory of phobias has been developing and a discussion of the current version of this account is provided in Chapter III. This theory is radically different from most of the prevailing theories which generally tend to regard phobic reactions as symbolic manifestations of some deeper, unconscious disturbance. For example, in Freud's famous case of Little Hans, the child's fear of horses was interpreted as a symbolic fear of his father combined with a fear of castration (see Wolpe and Rachman, 1961). The behavioral theory, on the contrary, regards phobias as maladaptive conditioned responses which have been acquired in a painful or excessively frightening situation.

This book describes the behavioral approach to phobias and their treatment. No attempt has been made to provide a general review of the topic or to evaluate other varieties of treatment. The scope of the book was deliberately restricted in an attempt to provide a concise account of what the author considers to be the most promising current approach to the problem of phobias.

Behavior therapy is a new development, and therefore most of the evidence and ideas discussed here are of recent origin. The main purpose of the book is to bring these developments to the attention of clinicians and research workers in the field of abnormal psychology.

CONTENTS

PHOBIAS
Their Nature and Control

Chapter I

THE NATURE OF PHOBIAS

A PHOBIA IS AN excessive fear reaction which is both persistent and unadaptive. When a phobic person is exposed to the fear-evoking stimulus or situation, a strong emotional reaction is produced. This reaction can be analyzed into three components: subjective, autonomic and motor.

The subjective aspect of a phobic response is experienced by the person as an alarming feeling of intense fear, tension or full panic, and is expressed in a variety of ways. Some patients, for example, will report they feel as if they are dying. Others feel they are suffocating; yet others that they are going to faint or collapse.

The autonomic reaction will include one or more of the following physiological changes: rapid respiration, sweating, trembling, palpitations, muscular tension and/or weakness, "butterflies in the stomach," involuntary excretion, breathlessness, nausea, dryness of the mouth. The motor response is usually one of flight but some patients become inert or "frozen" and feel too weak to move. Patients who experience these feelings of muscular weakness seek the support of another person, a wall or similar aids.

Theoretically, the stimuli or situations which can provoke a phobic reaction are infinite, but in practice there are a few which are encountered frequently. The most common phobias are claustrophobia, agoraphobia, acrophobia, animal phobias, interpersonal phobias, death-disease-injury phobias, sexual phobias. The following examples have been chosen to illustrate the three components as they occur in common phobias.

CASE 1: This patient was a forty-five-year-old married man diagnosed as suffering from severe chronic agoraphobia. The symptoms had begun ten years earlier. The patient complained primarily of an inability to walk about in public freely and of his fear of being alone. When he attempted to leave his home unaccompanied, he experienced a very severe anxiety reaction which he described as a feeling that "something dreadful was about to happen" to him. He had in fact experienced a number of panic attacks during which he felt that he was going to die (of a heart attack). The autonomic reactions which accompanied these subjective feelings of apprehension included breathlessness, palpitations and feelings of general weakness which forced him to support himself against the nearest wall. On the motor side, he tended to avoid a large number of situations, and when he was induced by pressing demand to leave his home, he restricted his walking to those routes which he knew contained walls on which he could support himself. It meant in fact, that whenever he walked outside his home he tended to creep alongside a wall, touching it as he proceeded.

Case 2: This patient was a claustrophobic woman of thirty-two. Subjectively, she reported that during the anxiety attacks she felt terrified of suffocating. The autonomic reactions which accompanied these feelings were palpitations, muscular weakness, a throbbing headache, nausea, dryness of the mouth. Her motor reaction when these feelings arose was one of escape. She described a number of occasions when she had been forced by her anxiety to escape from cinemas, churches and other enclosed places. On those occasions when she had been unable to escape rapidly, the feelings of weakness intensified and she felt that she was about to faint or to die.

Case 3: This patient was a seven-year-old boy who complained of an intense beephobia which had been disturbing him for the past two years. He described the subjective aspect of his reaction very simply as follows: "I am very frightened of the bees and feel scared that they will sting me and hurt me." His mother described the autonomic reaction which her child experienced when confronted with a bee: "He used to go white, sweaty, cold and trembling, and his legs were like jelly." The child's motor reaction was a combination of flight and total avoidance. This apparently simple and unimportant phobia had, in fact, severely curtailed the child's range of movement. For example, he was unable to play out-of-doors during the summertime and had to be driven to and from school during the spring and summer. On a number of occasions, however, he had been unable to avoid coming into contact with bees and these experiences had produced very sharp fear reactions. It was these intense reactions, in fact, which prompted the parents to seek treatment for the boy as they had undergone a number of very disturbing experiences with the child when he had been attempting to escape from bees. On at least two occasions he had run across busy streets when confronted by a bee and his parents were worried that he might come to harm because of his intense and sudden escape reactions.

CASE 4: A medical student complained of an intense fear of authority figures and examination situations. He described his feelings in the presence of authority figures (his teachers, senior colleagues, policemen, etc.) as one of total fear, sometimes bordering on panic. He reported that he was quite unable to cope with these people, and that when it was impossible for him to avoid a direct meeting with them, he felt extremely frightened and trembled openly. In his case, the autonomic reactions were primarily sweating, muscular tension, palpitations and a strong flush. In addition, the muscular tension quite often centered on the muscles of the throat region, and this prevented him from speaking normally in the presence of authority figures. His motor reaction was one of avoidance. Whenever and wherever possible, he avoided coming into contact with his teachers and senior colleagues. This unadaptive behavior was interfering with his medical education, apart from the heavy burden which it imposed on him in day-to-day matters.

In the last ten years a number of attempts have been made to describe and explain the phenomena of human phobias in terms of modern psychological knowledge. In 1960, Wolpe and Rachman proposed that phobic disorders can best be regarded as conditioned fear (anxiety) reactions and offered this definition: "Any neutral stimulus, simple or complex, that makes an impact on an individual at about the time that a fear reaction is evoked, acquires the ability to evoke fear subsequently. If the fear in the original conditioning situation was of high intensity, or if the conditioning is repeated a good many times, the conditioned fear will show the persistence that is characteristic of neurotic fear; and there will be generalization of fear reactions to stimuli resembling the conditioned stimulus."

According to this view, phobias are anxiety states in which the focus of the anxiety-producing stimuli is sharpened. To quote Wolpe (1962), "The distinctive feature of a classical phobia is the presence of clearly ostensible sources of anxiety . . . a behaviouristic analysis aims at the liquidation of these sources in every case."

In monosymptomatic phobias, the trigger stimulus can be identified and specified in a reasonably precise manner, whereas in complex phobias, several types of stimuli are found to elicit the anxiety reaction. Nevertheless, in learning theory terms it is possible to regard most (if not all) anxiety states as complex, multiple phobias. Viewed in this way, anxiety states and phobias (and for that matter, many other neurotic disorders) are seen to share many important characteristics.

As phobias apparently share many characteristics with other types of neuroses, it is worth reviewing here the three-stage theory of the development of neurotic disorders which was proposed by Eysenck and Rachman (1965). They suggest that in the first instance a single traumatic event, or a series of subtraumatic events, produce strong unconditioned autonomic reactions, mainly of the sympathetic nervous system. These strong emotional reactions may themselves be sufficient to disorganize the person's behavior. However, unless the traumatic events or stresses are persistent, we might expect that most people would resume their normal way of behaving once the pressures have been lifted.

This is in fact what happens to most people in most circumstances involving stress. However, in a large number of cases, secondary conditioning takes place. Previously neutral stimuli become connected (associated) with the unconditioned stimuli which gave rise to the excessive emotional reaction (e.g., the sight of a dog is associated with his bark and bite). Thereafter, the conditioned stimulus, as well as the unconditioned stimulus, can produce the original emotional behavior — i.e., the *sight* of the dog now produces an emotional reaction. It is this conditioning process which underlies the development of neurotic behavior and phobias in particular.

Although there is satisfactory evidence that a single traumatic event may produce persistent neurotic behavior, it seems more probable that the majority of neurotic disorders are the consequence of repeated exposure to frequent subtraumatic events. In their account of the development of combat neuroses, Grinker and Spiegel (1945) found that neurotic breakdowns were precipitated by four types of experience (in combination or alone):

breakdowns caused by a single catastrophe; those caused by several specific traumata; those caused by a gradual accumulation of mild anxiety; and those caused by severe and long-lasting anxiety.

Conditioned responses which are not reinforced begin to fade and extinguish. We would therefore expect that conditioned autonomic responses of the type described above would extinguish as and when the person repeatedly encounters the conditioned stimulus and it is not followed by reinforcement (pain or discomfort).

To continue with the simple example of a dog phobia, we may expect that even after the person has developed a fear reaction to the sight of a dog, he will inadvertently encounter them. If these encounters are not followed by pain or discomfort, the fear will weaken, fade and extinguish. If we are correct in assuming that fear and anxiety reactions are subject to natural extinction, we might then expect that the majority of neurotic reactions should show what is called *spontaneous remission,* and there is indeed a good deal of evidence to suggest that a large number of neurotic behavior patterns do in fact remit in the ordinary course of events (see Eysenck and Rachman, 1965; Eysenck, 1966).

It is still necessary, however, to explain why not all cases of neurotic disorder remit spontaneously. In order to encompass the persistence of some neurotic behavior patterns, Eysenck and Rachman suggest that there is a third stage in the development of these disorders. Once a person has acquired a neurotic reaction to a particular stimulus or class of stimuli, it will lead to a tendency for him to avoid these noxious or potentially disturbing situations. If the person is successful in avoiding exposures to the fear-producing stimuli, he will thereby "protect" himself from the possibility of natural extinction occurring. Conditioned responses are diminished in strength and eventually extinguished as a consequence of repeated and unreinforced evocations.

Where a person with a neurotic reaction is successful in avoiding contact with the phobic stimuli and situations, he is, of course, avoiding disturbing and unpleasant experiences, but paradoxically, he is also preserving the unadaptive, conditioned emotional reaction from being eroded. If our hypothetical patient with a fear of dogs is entirely successful in avoiding encounters with these animals, his fear reaction will remain unchanged. Thus, Case 1, described previously in this chapter, remained agorophobic precisely because of the restricted mobility which he imposed on himself in order to avoid unpleasantness. In a similar way the young boy (Case 3) with a fear of bees, by deliberately avoiding contact with bees, was unknowingly ensuring that the bee-phobic reaction was preserved from extinction.

Eysenck and Rachman argue that the three-stage theory which they have developed is particularly applicable to those disorders which are described as "dysthymic, i.e., to phobic reactions, anxiety states, obsessional and compulsive disorders, and so forth; these may be called disorders of the first kind, and our general hypothesis is that they are caused by conditioned autonomic fear responses and the reactions, skeletal, muscular and hormonal of the organism of these conditioned responses."

They distinguish between these disorders and a *second* group of disorders which are characteristic of extroverted personality types. In this second type of disorder the problem arises because of a failure of the conditioning process. The maladaptive behavior is a consequence of the person having failed to acquire the necessary, adaptive responses in the correct way and at the appropriate time.

Two examples of this type of disorder are psychopathic behavior and enuresis. In the case of psychopathic behavior, it can be said that the maladaptive behavior problem arises because the person has failed to acquire the appropriate conditioned anxiety reactions in situations where it is necessary for him to anticipate discomfort or pain as a consequence of his antisocial actions.

Eysenck and Rachman also propose an explanation for the *development* of these two different classes of disorder. They attribute the differences in development to two factors: individual differences in past learning and experience, and individual differences in hereditary disposition. They point out that all people differ with respect to their past learning experiences, and in particular, their exposures to appropriate and effective conditioned-anxiety situations.

This is merely another way of saying that a person's behavior is a reflection of his past experiences and someone who has been subjected to severe or prolonged stress is more likely to develop maladaptive emotional reactions than someone who has been, in this sense at least, sheltered. The second type of disorder such as is observed in psychopaths is a consequence of the person having been "sheltered" from exposure to effective social disapprobation and other negative consequences of unacceptable behavior.

In regard to the second major factor which produces these differences between the two types of disorder, there is little doubt that individual organisms "differ innately with respect to many variables which may determine the responses to several classes of stimuli . . . it is perhaps a little unfashionable to stress the importance of innate hereditary factors in behaviour, but the evidence regarding their importance is quite conclusive" (Eysenck and Rachman, 1965).

The authors also make an attempt to link up the two classes of neurotic disorder with Eysenck's two-dimensional model of personality. According to this scheme, the two major dimensions along which personality can be viewed are extroversion-introversion along the one scale and neuroticism on the other scale, and at right angles to the first.

This two-dimensional scale has been the subject of a great deal of research and there is a considerable evidence to support it. It will be recalled that the "typical extrovert" is outgoing, sociable, impulsive, optimistic, and so on. The "typical introvert," on the other hand, is a quiet, introspective, cautious and serious person.

The second major dimension, neuroticism, is akin to the description given by many other authors of emotional stability or instability. On the one hand, there are people whose emotional reactions are labile, intense and easily aroused. At the other extreme, there are people whose emotional reactions are more stable, weaker and more difficult to arouse. According to this view, neurotics would be expected to display the unstable type of reaction pattern.

This scheme is illustrated in Figure 1. It can be seen from the diagram that patients suffering from anxiety, obsessional disorders, phobias and the like fall into the top left-hand section of the neurotic-introvert quadrant. These people are introverted and emotionally labile. The neurotic-extrovert types fall into the top right-hand quadrant and typically develop psychopathic or hysterical disorders.

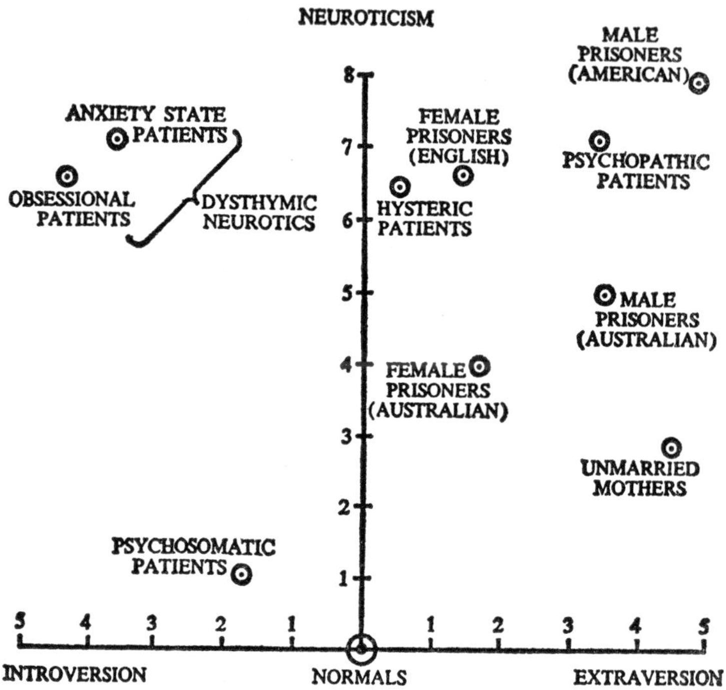

FIGURE 1. The dimensions of personality according to Eysenck's theory. The position of various neurotic and criminal groups on two factors of neuroticism and introversion-extroversion. Reproduced from Eysenck and Rachman (1965).

Figure 1 shows the results of analyses carried out in a number of different institutions and different countries over the past ten years. Although phobic patients are not described separately in any of the studies denoted in the Figure, they would, in terms of the research summarized here, fall into the group of anxiety-state patients as shown in the Figure.

In other words, the phobic patients can be expected to lie in the upper left quadrant — that is, neurotic and introvert. This links up with Eysenck's theory of personality in that introverts are said to be more readily conditionable than extroverts; consequently, exposure to fear-producing situations can be expected to be followed by the fairly rapid development of secondary conditioning.

The person begins to respond in a fearful way to stimuli which are inherently neutral but which have become capable of evoking fear as a consequence of a conditioned association developing. ". . . in our general system, introverts are postulated to condition more easily and, therefore, to acquire the conditioned anxiety and fears characteristic of the dysthymic more easily than other people, whereas psychopaths and prisoners generally are people who condition poorly and who, therefore, fail to acquire the conditioned responses characterising the process of socialization" (Eysenck and Rachman, 1965).

People do not only differ, however, in their predisposition to condition quickly or poorly, they also differ in another important respect. This second quality is described by the axis of neuroticism. It is argued that some people are innately predisposed to respond more strongly and more quickly to strong, painful or sudden stimuli. The dimension of neuroticism is "causally related to an excessive lability of the antonomic nervous system." The evidence for these innate individual differences is derived primarily from studies which have compared identical and non-identical twins, reared separately and apart. A full discussion of the biological basis of personality is provided in Eysenck and Rachman (1965) and by Eysenck (1967).

We can sum up this view of phobias as a type of neurotic disorder in the following way. It is possible to distinguish two broad categories of behavior disorder: dysthymic disorders and extrovert disorders. Phobias are dysthymic disorders and are found predominantly in that class of individuals who are introverted and high on neuroticism.

Phobias are most likely to develop in people who are innately predisposed towards introverted patterns of behavior, and are at the same time endowed with a labile autonomic nervous system. It can be expected that people who have this constitution will develop phobias earlier and/or more readily than either extroverts or people who are low on the neuroticism factor.

The theory also predicts that the majority of fearful reactions will tend to become extinguished in the natural way without recourse to any special procedures. Furthermore, the spontaneous remission rate in phobic and anxiety states should (with certain exceptions) be relatively high. The main exceptions can be expected to occur where the nature of the phobia enforces or permits a consistent pattern of avoidance behavior to develop.

For example, an agoraphobic person who is able to avoid making excursions will tend to show a chronic course of illness; where it is not possible for practical and other compelling reasons to restrict one's movements or to avoid leaving the safety of one's home, the agoraphobic's reactions can be expected to weaken and eventually extinguish. This distinction between the opportunities for avoidance in agoraphobia may help to account for the fact that it appears to be a phobia which is more common among housewives than among working males.

As the research and clinical work described in this book is approached in terms of this view of neurotic behavior, it is worthwhile to recapitulate the general theory. Phobias, like other neurotic disorders, develop in a three-stage process. In the first stage the person is exposed to traumatic events which produce strong emotional reactions. Stimuli associated with the events giving rise to the traumatic emotional reactions become conditioned signals which acquire the ability to produce the maladaptive emotional behavior, even in the absence of genuine threat or pain. The person's attempts to avoid exposure to these unpleasant fear reactions help to preserve the phobic reaction by ensuring that it is not subject to naturally occurring extinction through repeated and unreinforced exposures. When a person who has acquired an unadaptive fear reaction is of necessity brought into repeated contact with the fear-producing stimuli, one can expect a gradual weakening of the phobic reaction and its eventual disappearance.

Phobias are most likely to develop in introverted people who have a high degree of emotional lability (neuroticism). These people condition more easily than extroverts who tend to develop disorders other than anxiety states or phobias.

Chapter II

VARIETIES OF PHOBIAS

PHOBIAS CAN BE categorized in a number of different ways. They vary in complexity, duration and also in terms of the object which provokes the fear. Furthermore, it is necessary for certain purposes to distinguish between the phobias which occur mainly in childhood and those which are typical of adulthood.

COMPLEXITY

Phobias range from the very simple to the extremely complex, and as we shall see in a later chapter, there is good reason to believe that complex phobias require a greater therapeutic effort than simple ones. According to Wolpe (1964), "a patient may be regarded as having a simple neurosis if he has only one such habit (persistent, unadaptive anxiety) and if it consists of responses to a single and obvious family of stimuli." Examples of simple neuroses are dog phobias, snake phobias and certain instances of claustrophobia.

In their analysis of the effects of desensitization, Hain, Butcher and Stevenson (1966) mention several patients with monosymptomatic phobias. Patient No. 1 had an elevator phobia, No. 5 had a fear of social occasions, No. 16, a phobia about germs, and so on. Similarly, Wolpe (1961) mentions some patients with simple phobias — for example, Patient No. 6 had a phobia for crowds, Patient No. 7 had a fear of criticism, Patient No. 12 had a phobia of being watched while working, Patient No. 19 feared authority figures, Patient No. 25 feared rejection, and so on.

There is good reason to believe that simple phobias occur quite frequently in the general population and are tolerated by most people unless and until the fear begins to interfere with their normal activities. It is rare for someone to seek psychiatric treatment for a fear of mice or rats or cats, for example. Nevertheless, as some recent surveys have shown, these simple fears are comparatively widespread in the normal population (see Geer, 1965).

Phobias tend to become a psychiatric problem only when they are complex and their effects produce some measure of incapacitation. Examples of complex fears can be found in the report by Hain *et al.* (1966).

Patient No. 12, for example, complained of anxiety attacks, travel phobias, fear of social occasions, fear of public speaking, paroxysmal tachycardia. Patient No. 3 complained of a fear of hostility, a sex phobia, an excessive fear of girls, a phobia of criticism. Some of the complex phobias mentioned by Wolpe (1961) include the following: Patient No. 1 complained of claustrophobia, fear of illness and hospitals, fear of death and its associations, fear of storms, fear of quarrels. Patient No. 13 complained of a fear of suffering, a fear of being devalued and a fear of failing to come up to expectations.

A phobia can be regarded as complex for a number of different reasons. In the examples quoted above, the complexity was caused primarily by the fact that the patients had several interrelated fears. This multiplicity of fear-reactions is probably the most important contributor to phobic complexity, but there are other types of complexity as well.

One of the most difficult types to come to grips with and to treat is the condition which is sometimes described as *pervasive anxiety*. In these cases the person reports that he is anxious in a large range of situations and for most of the day. Even persistent interviewing, analysis and reanalysis fails to isolate any common themes running through the situations in which the person experiences excessive fear.

Phobic complexity may also arise because the person has, in addition to the excessive fear, a number of other psychiatric difficulties which may or may not be related to the phobia itself. The coexistence of several types of psychiatric disorder may obscure the presence of the phobia, or in certain instances, the presence of the phobia obscures other psychiatric difficulties.

Perhaps the most important of these coexisting or interlocking psychiatric disorders (from a clinical point of view, at least) is the combination of depression and phobia. In a number of cases it has been observed that the phobia appears to increase or diminish in an inverse relationship to the degree of depression which is present at any particular time.

From the theoretical point of view, it is perhaps best to reserve the term *complex phobia* for those conditions in which the person is subject to a number of different fears which are to some extent interdependent. From a practical point of view, it is important for the therapist to ascertain as best he can the degree of interdependence between the different phobias; the design and execution of the treatment program will of course be strongly influenced by the therapist's judgment on this matter.

If he concludes that the various phobias are quite independent, then his choice of the initial target is merely a matter of priorities. Which phobia should he attempt to treat first? However, when the phobias appear to be interdependent, then the therapist has to assess the *relative severity* of each type of phobia and make a treatment program which will integrate the different fear dimensions. In doing so, however, it is sometimes difficult to determine the comparability of the different types of phobia.

DISTANCE

In attempting to quantify the operations of desensitization treatment, Wolpe (1963) found it useful to incorporate the dimension of *distance* in his analysis of the progress of treatment in phobic conditions. He observed that in certain types of phobia, the early response to treatment is rapid and is then followed by a comparatively slow progression as the phobic object is approached. In other phobias, he observed that in the early stages of treatment, progress was apparently slow but once the patient had "begun to move," the treatment effects were accelerated.

The first type of phobia is called a *proximation phobia* and refers to those conditions in which the anxiety or fear-reaction increases with decreasing distance from the fearful object or situation. The second type of phobia is one in which the anxiety or fear-reaction increases with decreasing space and/or freedom of movement (e.g., claustrophobia).

A third type of phobia is one in which the fear increases with increasing distance from safety. These phobias, which are typified by agoraphobia, are referred to as *remoteness phobias.* The fourth type of phobia is one in which the phobic reaction increases with the number of fear-producing objects involved.

On the basis of his clinical observations, Wolpe observed that in the first two types of phobia (i.e., proximation and space phobias), fairly rapid progress is made in the early sessions of treatment. On the other hand, those phobias which increase with distance from safety (remoteness phobias) and those in which the fear increases with the number of phobic objects, the early response to treatment tends to be gradual and slow. This phase is then followed by rapid improvement after the first hump has been overcome. The response to treatment observed in these different types of phobia is discussed in a following chapter.

SITUATIONAL AND OBJECT PHOBIAS

Marks and Gelder (1966) carried out a retrospective examination of the varieties of phobia presented by 139 unselected patients. They made the interesting observation that none of the eighteen patients who complained of specific animal phobias had acquired the abnormal reaction in adult life, even though they only sought treatment in adulthood. Most of these specific phobias, (e.g., fear of birds, cats, dogs, etc.) had started before the age of five (see Table I). Situational phobias (e.g., fear of darkness, thunderstorms, etc.) showed a spread of onset age with some starting before five years of age and the majority beginning in adulthood.

They also did a separate analysis of what are described as *social anxieties* (e.g., phobias of eating in public, going to dances, etc.) and found that these tended to start after puberty. A separate analysis of agoraphobia revealed that this disorder started at any time "from late childhood to middle life, but with a bimodal distribution showing peaks at late adolescence and around the age of thirty."

It follows from their analysis that the phobias which have the longest history are those which involve a specific fear of animals. There is also some evidence that these phobias respond rather well to behavioral treatment (see Cooper, Gelder and Marks,

1965). The observation concerning the natural history of specific animal phobias made by Gelder, taken in conjunction with the gratifying response to treatment shown by patients with animal phobias, indicates in a very striking way the inadvisability of attempting to make a simple identification between the duration of a phobic disorder and its severity or prognosis. Marks and Gelder also point out that the simple animal phobias, in addition to having a different age of onset, are unlike the other phobias in showing a relatively continuous course of development and also because they are seldom associated with other psychiatric disorders.

TABLE I
AGE OF PATIENTS (IN YEARS) AT TIME OF ONSET OF PHOBIA AND AGE AT TIME OF TREATMENT

Type of Phobia	*N*	*Age at Onset* *Mean*	*SD**	*Age at Treatment* *Mean*	*SD*	*Symptom Duration Mean*
I. Specific animate	18	4.4	2.8	29.8	7.5	25.4
II. Specific situational	12	22.7	16.0	36.3	9.2	8.6
III. Social anxieties	25	18.9	8.3	26.8	6.5	7.9
IV. Agoraphobia	84	23.9	9.7	32.3	10.3	8.4

*SD = Standard deviation.
Reprinted from Marks and Gelder (1966).

As we shall see presently, fears of animals are fairly common in childhood but show a very high spontaneous remission rate. The problem which now requires explanation is why some adults, exemplified by these patients, fail to overcome their specific (animal) fears in the natural course of events. In what way are they unlike their peers? According to Eysenck's dimensional theory of personality, these children can be expected to possess a heightened predisposition to emotional instability (high neuroticism) and to acquire conditioned responses easily and rapidly (a central feature of introversion).

It would seem to follow from the analysis provided by Marks and Gelder that the situational phobias are more complex, and there is some evidence, although not definitive, that these phobias do not respond as readily to behavior therapy as do the specific animal phobias. They point out that the agoraphobic patients were the most handicapped of all and also the most difficult to treat. Agoraphobia was commonly associated with other psychiatric symptoms, notably general anxiety, depressions and obsessions.

FEARS IN CHILDHOOD AND ADULTHOOD

Broadly speaking, children and adults fear different objects and situations. Judging from a survey carried out on nonpsychiatric subjects (students), Geer (1965) observed that the most common fears among adults concerned the death of a loved one, public speaking, failure, suffocating, looking foolish, and so on.

Among young children, however, a different pattern of fears is observed. Jersild and Holmes (1935) reported that young children, unlike adults, tend on the whole to fear tangible objects (e.g., real animals and noises, etc.). Jersild and Holmes also noted that the fears of young, normal children are extensive. With increasing age, the number of fears declines and the quality of the fears also change. As they grow older, children learn to fear intangible situations, such as social rejection.

These developmental findings were substantiated to a large extent by MacFarlane *et al.* (1954), in their survey of some two hundred normal children, while Lapouse and Monk (1959) reported findings similar to those observed by Jersild and Holmes in the older age groups.

With increasing age, children tend to lose many of their fears. Jersild and Holmes, for example, plotted the decline of fears during the first four years of life (see Fig. 2). Similarly, MacFarlane plotted the percentage frequencies of various types of fear in normal children (see Fig. 3). It can be seen from MacFarlane's data that there is a fairly continuous decline in the number of fears reported between the ages of three and ten. At the age of eleven, however, there is a second peak — a finding also reported by Jersild and Holmes.

The decline of fears with increasing age was also illustrated in some experiments carried out by Holmes (1935). She exposed more than fifty children between the ages of two and six years to a variety of test situations involving potentially fearful stimuli. The percentage of children in whom fear responses were elicited by each of the situations is given in Table II. It will be seen that with the exception of snakes and large dogs, all the fears under study had disappeared by the age of five to six years.

TABLE II
PERCENTAGE OF CHILDREN SHOWING FEAR
IN EXPERIMENTAL SITUATIONS

	Percentage showing fear			
	2-3 yrs.	*3-4 yrs.*	*4-5 yrs.*	*5-6 yrs.*
I. Being left alone	12	15	7	0
II. Falling boards	24	9	0	0
III. Dark room	46	51	35	0
IV. Strange person	31	22	7	0
V. High boards	35	35	7	0
VI. Loud sound	22	20	14	0
VII. Snake	34	55	43	30
VIII. Large dog	61	43	43	12
Totals	32	30	18	5.2

Reproduced from Holmes (1935).

Dramatic declines in fear were observed in the test situations which involved a darkroom and, a loud sound. It is worth noticing, however, that the fear of snakes remained comparatively constant from one year to the next. The fear of dogs declined fairly markedly between the ages of two and five years but was not entirely absent at the age of five to six years.

This persistence of fear in regard to snakes and dogs is of some interest in view of the recent report by Marks and Gelder (1966) on the subject of adult phobias and their origins. They found that adult psychiatric patients who presented with monosymptomatic fears, especially of animals, said that they had had the fear since childhood. The evidence from the surveys of child development are consistent with this clinical observation in that a small minority of children retain their fear of certain kinds of animals throughout childhood.

Why certain people do not lose their animal fears during childhood is a problem which does permit a ready answer. However, it can be expected that these adults were more timid than their childhood peers and were possibly overprotected. These possibilities, however, will need to be examined in depth. In terms of Eysenck's theory, these people should fall into the dysthymic quadrant, i.e., show heightened neuroticism and introversion.

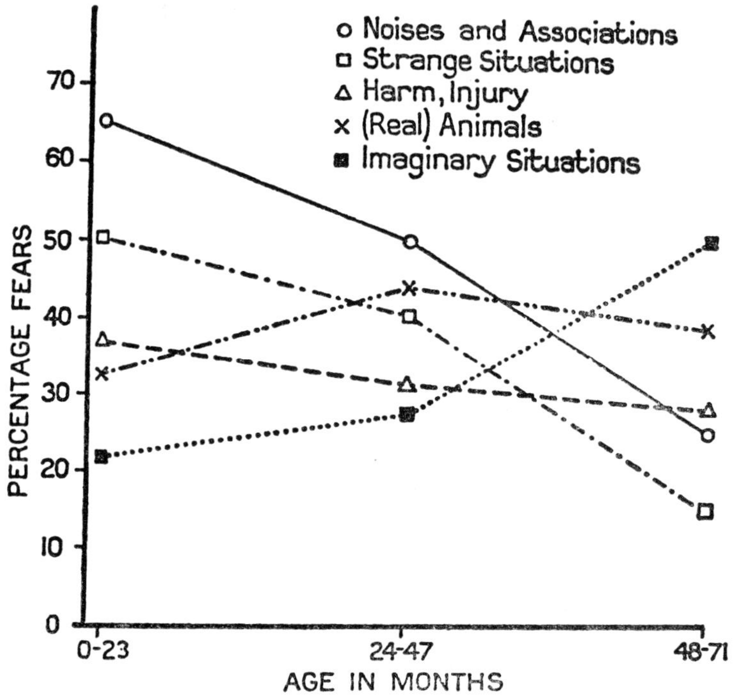

FIGURE 2. The relative frequency of fear responses in children of different ages. Reproduced from Jersild and Holmes (1935).

One such study is that reported by Slater (1939), who described the extinction of children's fears in a natural environment (nursery school). Forty children between the ages of two and three years were observed during the first four weeks of their attendance at school. During the first week, the majority of children displayed signs of uneasiness and apprehension. By the end of the fourth week, however, all but three of the children had adapted to the new situation successfully (see Fig. 4).

This study is an instructive example of the process of spontaneous remission, as well as an illustration of the parallel decline of the various overt behavioral manifestations of fear in young

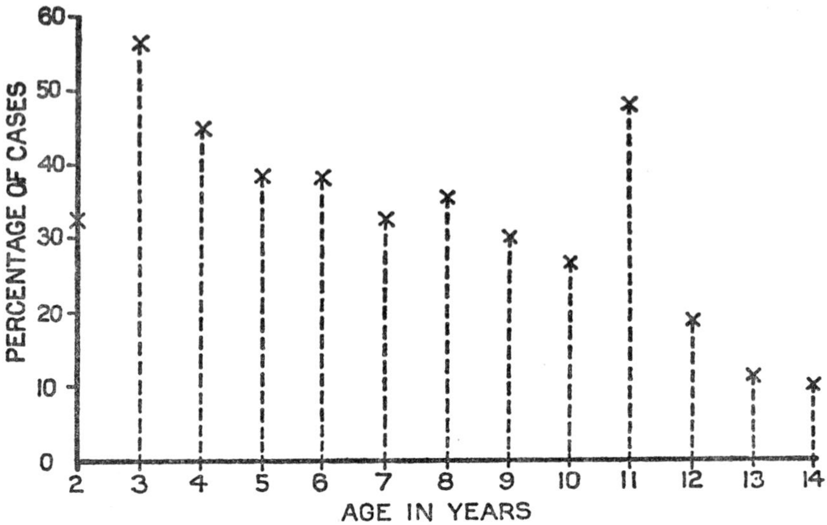

FIGURE 3. The fears of normal children. Adapted from Macfarlane *et al.* (1954).

children. It will be noticed from the figure that each of the observed signs declines most rapidly between weeks one and two, and thereafter gradually disappears over the course of the next two weeks.

The *deliberate* extinction or inhibition of fear in children was investigated by Jones in 1924. Apart from its inherent interest, this study has had a very considerable influence on the development of behavioral methods of treatment. Jones compared the effect of six different methods of overcoming fear in a group of children. Her conclusion was that of the six methods, only reconditioning and social imitation produced reliable successes. The reconditioning method which she employed would, in modern terms, be described as a process of reciprocal inhibition. The following case illustration indicates the method which she employed in the "imitation treatment" procedure.

> "A three-year-old boy, Peter, evinced fear of white rats, rabbits, fur, cotton wool, and other stimuli along this continuum." It was decided to concentrate on the rabbit phobia, as this appeared to be a focus of Peter's fears. The boy was gradually introduced to contacts

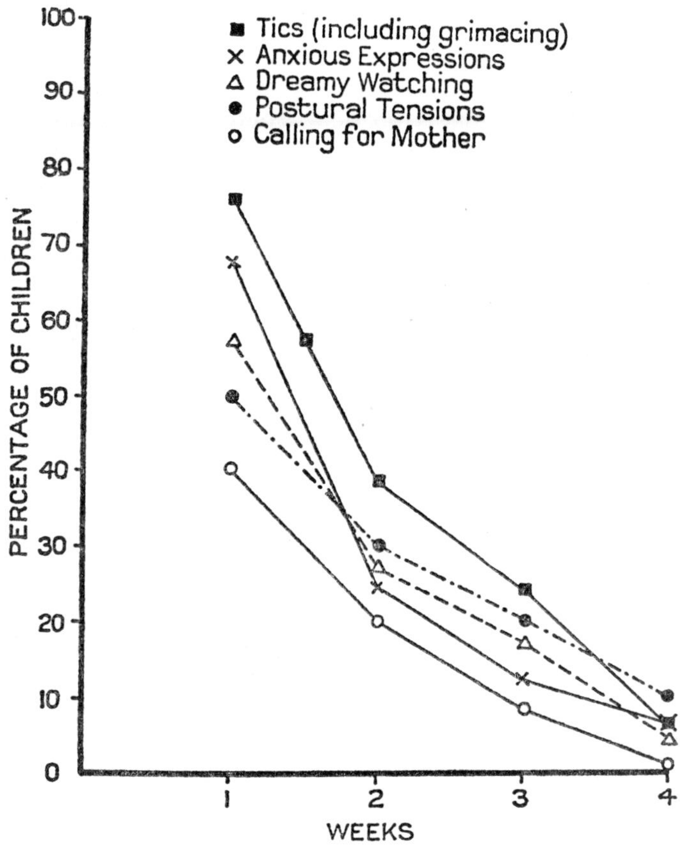

FIGURE 4. The extinction of children's fear responses in nursery school. Adapted from Slater (1939).

> with a rabbit during his daily play period. He was placed in a play group with three fearless children and the rabbit was then brought into the room for short periods each day. Peter's toleration of the rabbit gradually improved and the progressive steps used by Jones in this extinction process included the following. "Rabbit in cage 12 feet away tolerated . . . the cage four feet away tolerated . . . close by in cage tolerated . . . free in room tolerated . . . eventually, fondling rabbit affectionately."

This method of treatment by social imitation was recently the subject of a detailed experimental investigation and is discussed in a later chapter. The deconditioning method used by Jones involved the use of feeding responses. In this procedure the phobic stimulus was carefully and gradually re-presented to the child while he was eating. After he learned to tolerate the presence of the stimulus at a particular distance, it was then brought closer and closer to the child. This process of gradual desensitization was continued until the child could handle the animal without anxiety. "Through the presence of the pleasant stimulus (food) whenever the rabbit was shown, the fear was eliminated gradually in favour of a positive response" (Jones, 1924).

This combination of a gradual reexposure to the fearful stimulus and the simultaneous introduction of a pleasant and relaxing response (in this case, eating) provided a rudimentary model for Wolpe's "systematic desensitization" method.

FEAR-SURVEY SCHEDULES

Recent research into the nature and effectiveness of desensitization treatment has revived interest in the construction and use of fear-survey schedules. Most of the recent versions of these schedules were designed in response to the demands of the experimental studies of desensitization. For example, Lang and Lazowik (1963) developed a checklist of common fears and asked their subjects to rate the degree of fear which each item would produce in them. This schedule was then extended and revised by Wolpe and Lang (1964) in order to include a number of items which they regarded as being important in clinical investigations.

In all, they attempted to cover six different classes of fear-provoking stimuli in this Inventory. There are nine items dealing with animal phobias, seventeen dealing with social fears, eighteen dealing with illness, injury and death, four dealing with noises, sixteen dealing with classical phobias, and eight dealing with miscellaneous fears.

The typical animal phobias include snakes, worms, rats and so on. The social fears include being teased, people in authority, looking foolish, and so on. The illness and injury group include open wounds, dead people, injections, etc. The noise stimuli include loud noises, sirens, sudden noises, vacuum cleaners. The classical phobias include heights, darkness, large open spaces, travel, and so on. The miscellaneous items include strange places, failure, strange shapes, etc.

The Wolpe-Lang inventory contains seventy-two items, and as before, the patients are asked to rate the degree of fear which the objects or situations would provoke in them. The rating is made on a five-point scale which ranges from "not at all" to "very much." This list of seventy-two fear-provoking items was further extended to seventy-six items by Wolpe and Lazarus in 1966.

Another fear-survey schedule is that provided by Geer (1965). His inventory contains fifty-one items; the respondent is asked to rate his fear on a seven-point scale ranging from "none" to "terror." Geer's inventory was developed in a more formal way than those in which Wolpe was involved and he provides separate means for male and female students (total $n = 783$). The items in Geer's inventory are similar to those appearing in other schedules and the following items give some idea of the range covered: dead bodies, suffocating, looking foolish, hypodermic needles, blood, crowded places and so on.

Geer observed that women students reported more fears than men and that with very few exceptions their fears were more intense than those of the men. A fear of worms is more common in women, as is fear of rats and mice, fear of illness or injury to loved ones, and fear of seeing a fight. For the total sample, the most intense fears include: fear of the death of a loved one, fear of suffocating, fear of illness or injury to loved ones, fear of being self-conscious, fear of public-speaking.

Geer examined the Inventory's validity by exposing some of his subjects to *in vivo* avoidance tests in order to assess the relationship between their self-reported fears and their behavior in the presence of the actual object (e.g., dogs). The results obtained by this method were satisfactory. Other advantages of the Fear Schedule constructed by Geer are that an item analysis was carried out, normative means are provided and differences between the sexes are noted.

As the Wolpe-Lang and the Wolpe-Lazarus schedules have not yet been validated (Grossberg and Wilson, 1965) it seems preferable to use the schedule constructed by Geer. However, the Wolpe-Lazarus inventory contains a number of items which are of direct clinical relevance and which do not appear in Geer's list. For the present, therefore, it seems best to employ Geer's inventory for research investigation, but in the treatment of individual patients, the Wolpe-Lazarus list might be more productive.

In addition to the evidence provided by Geer, a number of other studies have examined the validity of subjective fear estimates (e.g., Walk, 1956, and Lanyon and Manosevitz, 1966). In brief, the evidence seems to indicate that subjective fear estimates provide a reliable but gross discrimination between people who are frightened of particular stimuli and those who are fearless. There are indications, however, that the finer differences reported by individual subjects cannot be relied upon – subjective reports regarding the intensity of the fear are not always borne out by the subject's behavior in the real-life avoidance test situation. For this reason the scales must be used with a degree of caution.

As has been suggested above, the Geer scale is preferable for research purposes and the Wolpe-Lazarus one for clinical needs. Naturally the best solution would be to develop and refine the Wolpe-Lazarus scale in order to provide greater accuracy and reliability in clinical work. These refinements should include the collection of norms for nonpsychiatric subjects and various groups of psychiatric patients. In addition, separate norms should be provided for men and women and for people of different ages.

Information about the reliability and validity of the scale should also be obtained. For purposes of illustration and possible use, the Geer inventory is reproduced in the Appendix. This scale was recently analyzed by Rubin, Katkin and Weiss (1967), who extracted four factors: fear of death and illness, fear of water, fear of interpersonal events, fear of concrete stimuli.

Chapter III

A THEORY OF PHOBIAS

In 1960, Wolpe and Rachman proposed a theory to account for the genesis and treatment of children's phobias. This theory has been through a few modifications (see Rachman and Costello, 1961; Eysenck and Rachman, 1965), and the present account is a development of these earlier versions. In essence, it is argued that phobias develop through a process of conditioning and that phobic reactions show the characteristics associated with other types of conditioned responses.

The experimental foundation for this theory is provided largely by laboratory studies on the production of artificial or experimental neuroses. An extensive account of the evidence on this subject is provided by Broadhurst (1960). The present discussion deals primarily with those experimental findings which appear to be relevant to phobias.

The laboratory research on experimental neuroses has in fact provided some important pointers in our attempts to establish a scientific explanation of the nature, causes, course and management of phobias. For example, Wolpe's definition of neurotic behavior arises to a considerable extent from his observations of experimentally induced neurotic behavior. According to him, neurotic behavior can be defined as persistent, unadaptive responding in which anxiety plays a central role. Certainly the majority of the reports on experimental neuroses lend themselves to this definition.

The characteristics of neurotic behavior as they have been observed in the laboratory include, among other things: excessive irritability, whining, defensive reactions, immobility, motor malfunctioning, and a host of other abnormal and bizarre types of reaction. It is also quite clear from this work that neurotic behavior is accompanied by abnormal physiological changes — these have been found to include abnormal respiratory functioning, excessive gastric acidity, heightened pulse and heart rates, maladaptive or totally impaired sexual responding (see Gantt, 1944; Anderson and Parmenter, 1941; Liddell, 1944).

The persistence of experimentally induced neurotic behavior is attested to by the work of Gantt, Wolpe (1958) and Masserman (1943), among others. One of the experimental animals described by Gantt remained neurotic from the beginning of the experiments (when the animal was two years old) until his death some six or seven years later. The unadaptive quality of neurotic behavior is exemplified by the refusal of neurotic animals to eat in the presence of a phobic stimulus even when they had been deprived of food for as long as seventy-two hours.

Anderson and Parmenter also provided evidence about the unadaptive nature of experimental neuroses when they described the way in which neurotic sheep who were previously gregarious become isolated, and instead of returning to the flock, kept well away from the other animals. The impairment of the sexual functioning is vividly described in the work reported by Gantt.

It is now evident that neurotic and phobic behavior can be induced in animals by one of the following three processes: Exposure to a serious conflict (perceptual, or one involving a clash of incompatible drives) can produce neurotic behavior (see Pavlov, 1927; Masserman, 1943); Exposure to a painful or fearful situation can produce neurotic and phobic reactions (Wolpe, 1958; Gantt; 1944); Subjecting an animal to "overstrain," or more broadly, excessive stimulation, can also produce neurotic breakdowns (Pavlov, 1927).

The probability of any one of these circumstances producing phobic or other neurotic behavior is decidedly enhanced if the animal is at the time of the exposure placed in a confined area (see Eysenck and Rachman, 1965). Apparently the factor of confinement contributes to the breakdown of behavior by preventing the animal from escaping, by restricting the conditioning to a limited number of cues, and by not allowing the animal to make a consistent response which might control the noxious stimulation.

It should be remembered that the factor of confinement is predominantly psychological (rather than physical) in character when it plays a role in the production of neurotic breakdowns in humans. Some interesting examples of the role played by *physical* confinement in the onset and maintenance of phobias in human beings are provided by Erwin (1963) who proposed the term *barber-shop phobia* as a description of the syndrome displayed by patients who panic when their movements are constrained.

The work on experimental neuroses has also shown the important role played by individual differences in determining the animal's resistance to breakdown. In addition, the type of neurotic behavior pattern which emerges when the animal's resistance does break down is largely determined by temperamental factors. The significance of individual differences was first noted by Pavlov himself. He distinguished between two major types of behavior disorder: inhibitory and excitatory disorders.

The early findings of Pavlov were replicated and extended by the Cornell group (Liddell, 1944; Anderson and Parmenter, 1941). The last-named authors provide excellent examples of each type of disorder. The inhibitory neuroses are typified by unadaptive immobility and motor retardation. The excitatory neuroses are characteristically exemplified by excessive activity, hyperkinesis and extreme irritability. The most plausible explanation for these individual differences is that they are constitutionally present and genetically determined. This interpretation has now received a good deal of support from twin studies which have been carried out over the past two decades. There seems to be little doubt that people and animals are predisposed to a greater or lesser extent to develop neurotic breakdowns. There is also a measure of evidence to suggest that the type of breakdown is largely determined by the person's hereditary endowment (see Eysenck and Rachman, 1965; Shields, 1964, and numerous other workers).

The animal research has also provided some extremely useful information about the efficacy of various types of treatment. It became clear from Pavlov's work, subsequently substantiated by the Cornell studies, by Gantt, Masserman and others, that the use of simple rest was a relatively useless procedure. Most of Pavlov's efforts were directed at attempts to treat the artificially induced neurotic disorders by drugs, bromides in particular. The results were not particularly encouraging and seemed to indicate that the use of sedative drugs can at best produce temporary alleviations of the neurotic condition. Similar conclusions were reached in the studies reported by the Cornell group, Masserman and others.

The indications are that the most effective way of treating neurotic behavior is to employ relearning or reconditioning procedures such as those described by Wolpe and by Anderson and Parmenter. In fact, the most widely used and best established of all the techniques of behavior therapy (desensitization) was developed in its essentials from Wolpe's attempts to treat neurotic cats. His research work led him to believe that a reconditioning or deconditioning procedure which was carried out in a gradual way on the basis of reciprocal inhibition, was the most promising basis for developing a psychotherapy based on the findings and methods of experimental psychology.

Another important contribution to the development of behavior therapy was made by the experimental work of Watson (1920) and Jones (1924). In association with Rayner, Watson provided a classical demonstration of the development of a phobia in a young child. Having first ascertained that it was a neutral object, Watson and Rayner presented an eleven-month-old boy, Albert, with a white rat to play with. Whenever Albert reached for the animal, the experimenter made a loud noise behind him. After only five trials Albert began showing signs of fear in the presence of the white rat. This fear then generalized to similar stimuli, such as furry objects, cotton wool, white rabbits. These phobic reactions were still present when Albert was tested four months later.

Watson and Rayner's demonstration made it clear that phobias can be generated by a simple conditioning procedure in which previously neutral stimuli are associated with painful or frightening stimuli in such a way as to "infect" the neutral stimulus. Here the neutral stimulus (the white rat) acquired the fear-producing property of the loud noise, and it was also noted that Albert's acquisition of a phobic reaction spread automatically to other stimuli which resembled the white rat in some manner (stimulus generalization).

Prompted by Watson's demonstration, Jones (1924) carried out a series of therapeutic experiments with phobic children. Her results suggested that the most effective ways of reducing or eliminating phobias in children were deconditioning and/or the use of imitative responses. In the deconditioning procedure, the phobic stimulus was gradually brought closer and closer to the child while he was eating — the aim was to inhibit fear responses by superimposing the positive, parasympathetic feeding responses upon the noxious ones. As will become evident in a later chapter, Jones's procedure was influential in the development of the behavioral technique known as desensitization.

A THEORY OF PHOBIAS

1. Phobias are learned responses.
2. Stimuli develop phobic qualities when they are associated temporally and spatially with a fear-producing state of affairs.
3. Neutral stimuli which are of relevance in the fear-producing situation and/or make an impact on the person in the situation are more likely to develop phobic qualities than weak or irrelevant stimuli.
4. Repetition of the association between the fear situation and the new phobic stimuli will strengthen the phobia.
5. Associations between high-intensity fear situations and neutral stimuli are more likely to produce phobic reactions.
6. Generalization from the original phobic stimulus to stimuli of a similar nature will occur.
7. Noxious experiences which occur under conditions of excessive confinement are more likely to produce phobic reactions.
8. Neutral stimuli which are associated with a noxious experience (S) may develop (secondary) motivating properties. This acquired drive is termed the fear drive.
9. Responses (such as avoidance) which reduce the fear drive are reinforced.
10. Phobic reactions can be acquired vicariously.

Clinically, it is often difficult to determine the origin of a patient's phobia. In planning and executing behavioral treatment such information can be very useful even though it is not essential. From the theoretical point of view, however, the nature and timing of the trigger event or events is of considerable importance. Any attempt to explain the genesis of phobic disorders must provide answers to the following types of questions. Can a single unpleasant experience cause a phobia? What sort of experiences can provoke a phobia? Can phobias develop as a consequence of imitation? How is it possible for someone to fear an object or situation which he has never come into contact with?

There are a number of examples of what is called *one-trial learning* in the literature on experimental psychology. Sanderson *et al.* (1963) produced an intense fear reaction in their human subjects by submitting them to one harrowing experience. Gantt *et al.* (1962) were also able to demonstrate one-trial learning in an experiment involving a group of dogs. In both of these experimental investigations, the unconditional stimulus was traumatic and the conditioned responses which emerged were extremely resistant to extinction. Some of the subjects in the Sanderson experiment actually showed an increase in the magnitude of their fear reaction with the passing of time, even though they were not reexposed to the traumatic stimulation. This unreinforced growth and expansion of the fear reaction was a little surprising, and may be of some importance in accounting for the persistence of certain types of strong fear.

Some observational evidence which also suggests the occurrence of one-trial learning of fear was obtained by Woodward (1959). She found that 81 per cent of 198 children who had suffered severe burns showed "signs of emotional disturbance according to their mothers" from two to five years after the accident. The most prominent symptom manifested by these children was "fear and anxiety." A comparison of these children with their siblings showed a marked difference between the two groups. Only 7 per cent of the siblings showed symptoms of fear and anxiety. It seems reasonable, therefore, to entertain the idea that a phobia might be generated by a single traumatic experience.

Clinically, one sometimes encounters a patient who can date the onset of a phobia to a specific experience at a precise time. More often, however, it is difficult to pin down the exact point at which it started and the nature of the precipitating event is not always clear.

On the basis of clinical observation and laboratory experimentation, it seems more probable that the great majority of traumatically induced phobias develop after a number of exposures to traumatic or subtraumatic experiences. Even in Watson's classical demonstration with Albert, five trials were necessary before the boy displayed fear in the presence of the neutral stimulus. In a replication of Watson's study, Jones (1937) confirmed the cumulative effect of repeated exposures to a painful or frightening situation (this cumulative effect has also been noted in experiments with animals).

According to Metzner (1961), repeated mild shocks "which by themselves do not elicit great emotional disturbance" can eventually produce neurotic behavior. It should be mentioned at this point, however, that under carefully controlled experimental conditions, the gradual and graduated exposure of animals to subtraumatic stimulation can lead to the acquisition of a type of immunity to later stresses (Miller, 1960). On the other hand, Kurtz and Walters (1962) and Walters (1963) have demonstrated that animals who are subjected to intensely fear-provoking experiences tend to react with increased fear when they subsequently encounter aversive stimuli. In these studies, prior exposure to fear-producing stimulation tended to weaken the animal's resistance to later stress, unlike the animals described by Miller. It should be remembered, however, that Miller was using a mild and gradual "desensitizing" procedure and *not* a series of randomly distributed and intense fear-producing experiences. The importance of repeated exposures to noxious stimulation lies mainly in the relationship between the frequency of such experiences and the *strength* of the fear. The mechanism which is thought to be primarily responsible for the *persistence* of the fear is the acquired secondary fear drive.

Basing their argument on some earlier work reported by Miller (1951), Eysenck and Rachman (1965) proposed that five major determinants contribute to the magnitude of a fear:

1. Repetition of exposures to the fear-inducing situation will increase the strength of the fear.
2. Strong noxious stimuli will produce strong fears (e.g., a powerful shock will produce greater fear than a weak one).
3. Stimuli which are closely associated, temporally and spatially, with a noxious experience will produce strong fears.
4. Generalized fear stimuli which resemble the original noxious stimuli closely will produce strong fears.
5. The summation of fear-inducing stimuli will increase the strength of the fear.

In 1939, Mowrer put forward the notion that fear might act as a learned, anticipatory response to painful stimulation. He argued that the presence of a conditioned pain response (fear) motivates the organism to escape, and those responses which bring about a reduction of the fear are reinforced or strengthened. This process can be illustrated by reference to the condition of agoraphobia. The patient experiences a frightening situation while in a public place (e.g., he feels that he is having a heart attack). On subsequent occasions he will again experience tension and discomfort when he approaches the area of the first anxiety attack.

This anticipation of a further unpleasant experience can be regarded as a conditioned anticipatory fear. The fear arises and increases whenever he enters the originally frightening situation, or indeed, any situation which resembles it. The mounting fear then impels the person to make various attempts to contain or eliminate the fear. The action which most often brings relief is a return to the safety of his home.

On his arrival home, the patient generally experiences a reasonably quick dissipation of the fear; this relief will tend to reinforce and strengthen his tendency to retreat on subsequent occasions. In other words, the response of returning home is reinforced because it is followed by a reduction of the fear drive. Later attempts to travel towards public situations will result in a reactivation of the fear drive, and again, returning home will reduce the fear drive and the behavior pattern of retreating is further reinforced.

Eventually, this process, if not checked, will restrict the person's movements to a narrow environment surrounding his home, or in extreme cases, make him entirely housebound.

Eysenck and Rachman (1965) attach critical importance to the role of the fear drive in maintaining phobic behavior. They argue that "neurotic behaviour patterns persist, paradoxically, because they are unpleasant. Once he has acquired an unpleasant reaction to a particular situation, the person then tends to avoid further contact with that situation. As learned patterns of behaviour can only be extinguished by repeated, unreinforced (or inhibited) evocations, the tendency to avoid the noxious situation often precludes the spontaneous disappearance of the neurotic behaviour."

Typically, phobic patients engage in carefully planned, evasive behavior in their determination to avoid coming into contact with the phobic object or situation. This avoidance behavior succeeds in suppressing the fear drive whenever it arises, but in so doing, the relief obtained has the retrospective effect of strengthening the avoidance behavior. This pattern has been described as a vicious circle which protects the conditioned fear response from the spontaneous erosion known as *extinction.* Curiously, phobic people who are unsuccessful in their attempts to avoid coming into contact with the phobic stimuli are more likely to experience a spontaneous remission of their fears than those people who are able successfully to avoid the possibility of experiencing even small amounts of discomfort.

It would appear then that although fear is *generated* by painful experiences, it is *sustained* by the operation of the secondary fear drive. This view is unfortunately not entirely satisfactory because there are some facts that it cannot apparently accommodate. Eysenck (1967) has recently drawn attention to the *Napalkov phenomenon,* according to which the effects of certain types of traumatic stimulation do *not* decrease over time.

Napalkov (1963) described an experiment in which dogs were

subjected to noxious stimulation and he reported the strange finding that after only one such exposure, the intensity of the fear reaction continued to increase despite the absence of further provocation. Instead of adapting to the repeated re-presentation of the conditioned stimulus, these dogs showed a gradual increase in the intensity of the fear reaction. The growth of the fear reaction continued for as long as five months, even though the dogs were kept in a kennel during this period.

This spontaneous deterioration is reminiscent of the experiment reported by Sanderson *et al.* (1963), in which their subjects showed an ever-widening conditioned fear reaction after only one exposure to an extremely traumatic situation. It also seems possible that the Napalkov phenomenon has its clinical counterpart; certainly there are some patients whose phobias appear to increase in intensity even when they have not been exposed to any obviously aggravating experiences. Eysenck suggests that this phenomenon might underlie the clinical observation that some patients present a history in which the original traumatic event was not followed immediately by a strong conditioned fear, but "where this fear seems to grow in time, so that exposure to the unreinforced conditioned stimuli does not seem to lead to extinction, but rather to an increase in the severity of the conditioned response." He also points out that a proportion of phobic patients do not show spontaneous remission and may even deteriorate with time in spite of the fact that no further reinforcement (i.e., pairing of the conditioned phobic stimuli and the unconditioned trigger stimuli) occurs.

The explanation of this mushroom effect is still obscure, but the curious failure to adapt, or to become habituated, may be of considerable theoretical and practical importance (see Ch. IV). It should be said, however, that the experiments reported by Napalkov will need to be replicated. His observations were limited to a small number of animals, and we have good reason to believe that there will be marked individual differences between animals and people who are studied in this way. The great variety of reactions which can be provoked by exposure to noxious stimulation and the individual differences in degree of resistance to stress have been amply demonstrated by the work of Pavlov (1927), Gantt (1944) and others. Unlike Napalkov's subjects, some of the animals described by these and other workers showed extraordinary powers of resistance despite the fact that they were exposed to a large number of different and intense types of stress.

THE VICARIOUS ACQUISITION OF FEAR

Clinicians frequently encounter phobic patients who cannot recall having undergone any traumatic experiences which may be associated with the object of their fear. Moreover, some patients (and nonpsychiatric subjects who have excessive fears of one type or another) complain that they have a phobia for certain situations or objects (e.g., poisonous snakes) which they almost certainly have never encountered.

For example, the student subjects treated by Lang and Lazowik (1963) for snake phobias were all living in Pittsburgh, and it would be unreasonable to suppose that each and every one of them had at some stage encountered a snake, or indeed, that there was any likelihood of their encountering a snake in the streets of Pittsburgh, at least not until Lang and Lazowik started their research. Nevertheless, they all complained of a genuine, excessive fear of snakes and these self-reports were confirmed by exposing the subjects to a live snake in the laboratory. The majority of these subjects probably acquired their fear of snakes by second, third or tenth remove.

It is worth remembering at this point an observation made by Jones (1925), who noted that children are less likely to develop fears when they are in the company of trusted and reassuring adults than when they are alone. Again, children are less likely to develop fears when they are in the presence of unafraid children than when they are with frightened children. The social facilitation or inhibition of fear was also noted by John (1941) in a study on the effects of air raids on children's behavior. It was found that the fear (or lack of fear) displayed by the child's mother was an important determinant of her child's fears.

There is, of course, a good deal of correspondence between frequency of fears of children of the same family — May (1950) reported correlations between the fears displayed by siblings ranging from 0.65 to 0.74. Similarly, Hagman (1932) found a correlation of 0.67 between the total number of fears exhibited by children and their mothers. The probability of a child acquiring fears by a process of social learning is directly influenced by the fears which he observes in his parents, siblings and friends.

Interest in the importance of imitation as a major process underlying the growth of social behavior has been revived by the persuasive work of Bandura and Walters (1963). Most of their studies have been concerned with the social transmission of aggressive behavior. However, Bandura (1965) has recently turned his attention to other types of behavior, including fear. He says, "In the case of vicarious classical conditioning, the observer's vicariously elicited emotional responses become conditioned through contiguous association to formerly neutral stimuli." He then gives a number of examples in which an observer who witnesses a model undergoing aversive conditioning begins to exhibit negative emotional reactions to the conditioned stimulus even though he himself has not experienced the aversive stimulation directly. Findings of this type leave little doubt that affective responses can be acquired through a process of imitation.

Bandura defines vicarious learning events as ones "in which new responses are acquired or the characteristics of existing response repertoires are modified as a function of observing the behaviour of others and its reinforcing consequences, without the modelled responses being overtly performed by the viewer during the exposure period." He argues that imitative responses are acquired and retained in the same way as other learned responses and are governed by the "traditional principles of associative learning such as frequency and recency, serial organization and multiple sources of associative interference."

Some of the factors which determine the acquisition of vicarious responses (presumably including fear) are the characteristics of the model, the characteristics of the observer, the relationship between the observer and the model, the extent of the observer's psychological arousal, the consequences of the model's behavior, and so on.

Bandura also makes it clear that responses are not only *acquired* vicariously; they can also be *inhibited* vicariously. An early example of the therapeutic use of social imitation is to be found in the work of Jones (1924), who found that this method was, in addition to reciprocal inhibition by feeding, the most effective procedure for reducing children's fears. Bandura has, in fact, recently reported a detailed investigation into the therapeutic effectiveness of imitation in overcoming a fear of dogs among nursery-school children (see Ch. VII).

SUMMARY

Human phobias are learned responses. They can be acquired by exposure to a single intensely painful or frightening situation, but are more probably acquired as a result of repeated exposures to subtraumatic situations. They can also be acquired as the result of exposure to conflict or by a process of imitation. Like other neurotic reactions, phobias can be regarded as persistent, unadaptive reactions which are strongly colored by the subjective, autonomic and motor manifestations associated with anxiety.

There are individual differences in the degree to which people are predisposed to develop phobic disorders (or more generally, neurotic disorders) and these differences show a marked genetic contribution. Phobias are generated either by exposure to stress or by imitation; they are maintained and persist because of the operation of the secondary fear drive which is reduced when the person retreats from or avoids the fear-provoking stimuli. The strength of a phobic reaction will be determined by the factors of frequency of exposure, intensity of the stimulation, temporal and spatial contiguity, degree of confinement and the summation with other fear-producing stimuli or situations.

Chapter IV

THE TREATMENT OF PHOBIAS: DESENSITIZATION

AT PRESENT, THE most effective method of treating phobic disorders appears to be *systematic desensitization.* This procedure is the most widely used of all the methods of behavior therapy and was derived from and is closely connected with experimental psychology. Moreover its operations and effects can be explicitly described and properly examined. On current evidence there seems little doubt that the technique is both logical and effective. There is a convincing collection of experimental results (see Ch. V) to support this view and clinical confirmation, although not yet entirely definitive, is well on the way.

Desensitization was developed by Professor Wolpe in the early 1950's. He arrived at this method, which may be described as a gradual deconditioning of anxiety responses, in the following manner. Dissatisfied with the results which he was obtaining with prevailing forms of psychotherapy, Wolpe returned to an examination of experimentally induced neurotic disturbances. At the time, two promising leads were those provided by the work of Pavlov and his successors on artificial neuroses, and the early but neglected work of Watson and of Jones on the genesis and elimination of children's fears.

Wolpe (1958) carried out a series of experiments on the artificial induction of neurotic disturbances in cats and came to the conclusion that the most satisfactory way of treating these neurotic animals was by a gradual deconditioning process along the lines proposed by Jones in 1924. It will be remembered that Jones discovered that one of the most effective ways of reducing or eliminating children's fears was to inhibit the unadaptive reaction by superimposing upon it an antagonistic (feeding) response.

With this work in mind, Wolpe started by feeding the neurotic cats in an environmental situation which was distinctly dissimilar from the original traumatic environment. He then proceeded gradually, through a series of carefully arranged stages, to situations which approximated more and more to the original traumatic situation. He found that in this way he was able to overcome the animals' neurotic reactions and restore them to apparent normality. It was obvious, however, that feeding responses would not be appropriate or indeed effective in the treatment of adult patients. His search for responses which would be antagonistic to anxiety lead him to the work of Jacobson (1938), who recommended the use of relaxation as a treatment for neurotic disorders of all kinds. Wolpe decided to substitute relaxation for feeding as the major incompatible response which would dampen the phobic and anxiety reactions.

As has been shown elsewhere (Eysenck and Rachman, 1965), there is ample data to show that the imposition of antagonistic responses (feeding, relaxation, etc.) upon anxiety will in definable circumstances reduce the intensity of the anxiety reaction.

At first he attempted to relax his patients in the presence of the actual anxiety-provoking objects or situations (*in vivo* desensitization). This method, he soon discovered, was both tedious and impractical. Furthermore, as some patients did not experience anxiety in the presence of discrete and tangible objects, it meant that he would either have to refuse such patients treatment or develop some new method. He then began experimenting with the imaginary evocation of the anxiety-producing stimuli and found that it provided an effective substitute for the real object or situation. In other words, instead of attempting to treat a patient complaining of a phobia of dogs with an accumulation of photographs and models of dogs, he simply asked the patient to imagine these objects while relaxing in a consulting room.

In the early development of this form of treatment, Wolpe relied heavily on hypnotic inductions — that is, the patient was first hypnotized and then asked to imagine the situation while under relaxation. It is now quite clear that the hypnotic procedure, while it may certainly abbreviate treatment, is not an essential part of the therapeutic method. In a recent publication, Wolpe and Lazarus (1966) report that approximately two thirds of their patients do not receive hypnotic training. The imaginary evocation of anxiety-producing stimuli under relaxation produced results, and Wolpe found that it was easy to manipulate the technique in a consulting room. It also allowed the therapist a high degree of flexibility in the planning of treatment.

Very simply, this is how the method of desensitization works. The patient is relaxed and then requested to imagine the anxiety-producing stimuli in a very mild and attenuated form. When the image is obtained vividly, a small amount of anxiety is usually elicited. The therapist then relaxes the patient again and instructs him to stop imagining the scene. The sequence is: relax – imagine – relax – stop imagining.

The superimposition of relaxation on the anxiety reaction produces a dissipation of anxiety (reciprocal inhibition). This process is then repeated with the same stimulus or with a stimulus which is slightly more disturbing. The patient is again relaxed and the next stimulus is then presented and dissipated. With each evocation and subsequent dampening of the anxiety response, conditioned inhibition is built up. Eventually the patient is able to imagine even the previously most anxiety-provoking stimulus with tranquility and this tranquility then generalizes to the real-life situation.

The transfer of improvements from the consulting room to the real situation usually accompanies each stage of the treatment program in a fairly regular fashion. When the person is able to envisage the previously disturbing stimuli in the consulting room without any anxiety, he generally finds that he is able to cope with the actual stimulus in a real-life situation without difficulty.

Naturally, before the systematic desensitization treatment proper commences, various preliminary steps have to be taken. In the first place, a full history of the patient's disorder and his general background are obtained. Secondly, an attempt is made to reduce or eliminate any conflicts or anxiety-provoking situations which are found to prevail at the time of treatment. If, for example, a patient's parents or spouse are exposing him to situations which produce anxiety, an attempt will be made to alter both their behavior and the patient's reactions (see Wolpe, 1958, for clinical examples). Thirdly, the therapist attempts to explain the rationale of the desensitization treatment and also gives him some idea as to the type of exercises which will be involved.

When these preliminaries (history taking, environmental changes, explanation of treatment procedures) have been completed, the treatment commences. Detailed accounts of the technique and its origin are provided by Wolpe (1958) (1961), Eysenck and Rachman (1965), Lazarus (1964), Paul (1966) and Wolpe and Lazarus (1966). A selection of cases is available in Eysenck (1960, 1964), Eysenck and Rachman (1965), Ullmann and Krasner (1965) and Wolpe (1958). For present purposes, an outline of the technique is given.

Like all the therapeutic procedures developed and employed by Wolpe, desensitization is based upon the following general principle: "If a response antagonistic to anxiety can be made to occur in the presence of anxiety-provoking stimuli so that it is accompanied by a complete or partial suppression of the anxiety responses, the bond between the stimuli and the anxiety responses will be weakened." (Wolpe, 1958).

For convenience we may divide the stages of desensitization treatment into four:

1. Preliminaries (history taking, etc.).
2. The patient is trained in progressive relaxation.
3. Hierarchies of phobic stimuli and/or anxiety-provoking situations are constructed and ranked in ascending order of intensity.
4. The patient is required to imagine the phobic stimuli in gradually ascending order while in a state of deep relaxation.

The method of relaxation which the patient is taught is an abbreviation of that developed by Jacobson in 1938. Ordinarily it takes three to six training sessions to bring the patient to the point where he can, with minimal instructions, achieve a reasonably deep state of relaxation.

Jacobson's method involves four stages: developing a "muscle sense," relaxing one muscle group (e.g., biceps) "further and further" until a tingling sensation develops, relaxing consecutive muscle groups separately, relaxing various groups of muscles simultaneously.

After the patient has been given some practice in achieving "muscle sense," various groups of muscles are flexed and then relaxed. This relaxation practice takes between twenty and thirty minutes, and the patient is also instructed to practice at home for two fifteen-minute sessions a day. Although there is no absolutely fixed sequence of relaxation training, it is most common to start with the arms and legs in the first session and then move to the muscles in the head and neck regions at the end of the first or at least the beginning of the second session. When the patient has successfully learned to relax each important group of muscles, an attempt is made to coordinate the relaxation of these disparate muscles and, ideally, he should respond with widespread relaxation on instruction. An important part of the relaxation training is slow regular breathing.

According to Jacobson, the features of deep relaxation are regular respiration, normal pulse rate, diminished knee jerk, relaxed esophagus, flaccid limbs, absence of reflex swallowing, motionless eyelids, absence of tremors, subjective sensations of pleasant restfulness. In clinical practice, the most telling overt signs of a successful induction of relaxation are bodily stillness, flaccid muscles, regular breathing, motionless eyelids, involuntary jerks (in the early stages of induction), slowness to respond, a report of sleepiness at termination of relaxation session.

It is not yet known for certain how thorough and extensive this training in relaxation must be in order to achieve reasonable therapeutic results. It is worth noticing that in a group of non-psychiatric subjects with an excessive fear of public speaking, Paul (1965) was able to achieve very encouraging results with a comparatively brief form of relaxation training. Detailed instructions for relaxation training are provided by Wolpe and Lazarus (1966, pp. 177-180) and by Paul (1965, pp. 115-122).

According to Wolpe and Lazarus, the construction of anxiety hierarchies is the "most difficult and taxing procedure in the desensitization technique . . . it requires accurate recognition of the stimulus sources of the unadaptive anxiety response, painstaking itemization and careful grading of items . . . an anxiety hierarchy is a graded list of stimuli incorporating different degrees of a defined feature that evokes anxiety."

Working from the patient's history and the information provided by various questionnaires and inventories, the therapist assists the patient in enumerating those stimuli and situations which provoke fear. The therapist then attempts to isolate the themes running through the patient's list of items and then to order them into a meaningful and graded series or hierarchy.

The procedure is illustrated by Wolpe and Lazarus in this way. After listing the initial fears described by a particular patient, they then proceeded to categorize the original twenty fears into five hierarchies. The original list of fears contain the following twenty items: high altitudes, lifts, crowded places, church, darkness, being alone, marital relations, walking any distance, death, accidents, fire, fainting, falling, injections, medications, fear of the unknown, losing my mind, locked doors, amusement-park rides, steep stairways. With the assistance of the patient, the items were then sorted out into the following hierarchies:

1. *Acrophobia* (high altitudes, amusement-park rides, steep stairways).
2. *Claustrophobia* (lifts, crowded places, church, darkness, locked doors).
3. *Agoraphobia* (being alone, walking any distance alone).
4. *Illness* (fainting, falling back, injections, medications).
5. *Basically objective fears* (marital relations — actually pregnancy, death, accidents, fire, fear of the unknown, losing my mind).

Among the common hierarchies encountered in treating phobic patients are claustrophobia, agoraphobia, social fears, fear of injury, fear of heights and sexual fears.

The third part of the treatment, the desensitization itself, is carried out as follows. The patient is told which stimuli are to be presented in the individual session and is advised to signal with his hand if a stimulus presentation disturbs him unduly. This is an important instruction and should not be omitted, because the arousal of excessive anxiety during a session can be very disruptive. With most patients it is possible by observing their facial expressions, bodily tensions, respiration and so on, to perceive such disturbances before the patient actually signals them. When such disturbances occur, the therapist immediately withdraws the stimulus and calms the patient. If, at the conclusion of a session, the "last" item produces a disturbance, the therapist must, before arousing the patient, present an easy stimulus which has already been overcome successfully.

In order to facilitate an easy exchange of information, the patient is instructed to use a "fear thermometer." The patient is taught how to rate the magnitude of his anxiety or fear reactions on a scale ranging from 0 (absolutely calm) to 100 (a feeling of total panic). Accordingly, a very mild reaction might be rated as 15 and a very intense one as, say 80. At various stages in the treatment the patient is asked to estimate the degree of disturbance which he experienced during the presentation of an imaginary stimulus situation by using the fear thermometer.

When the preliminary instructions have been given, the patient is then relaxed (hypnotically or otherwise) and told to visualize the various stimuli, e.g., "picture a hospital in the distance . . . now stop picturing that and go on relaxing." Each visualization of this kind is referred to as a presentation, and each stimulus is visualized for five to twenty seconds with from two to four items being presented in each session, depending on the patient's progress at the time. Each item is generally presented between two and six times, although there is some evidence that stimuli which produce intense reactions require a larger number of repetitions (Rachman, 1966).

When, during a session, the required number of stimuli have been presented, the patient is slowly aroused and asked for a full report on his reactions. If the items have been visualized vividly and without undue disturbance, the therapist then proceeds to the next stimuli in the following session. Each session is ordinarily commenced with a repetition of the last item presented in the previous session — this is to counteract the spontaneous reappearance of some measure of the fear reaction which sometimes occurs between sessions.

The items lowest in the hierarchy (i.e., the least-disturbing ones) are introduced first, and the therapist proceeds slowly up the list depending upon the progress achieved and the patient's reaction. In this way it is possible for the patient eventually to imagine formerly phobic and noxious stimuli without any anxiety whatever. As the purpose of this technique is to decondition anxiety and phobic reactions, it is necessary for the patient to experience some anxiety during the stimulus presentations. The total inhibition of the neurotic anxiety reaction is achieved by inhibiting small degrees of anxiety in this gradual and systematic progression.

The desensitization technique is illustrated in a case report presented by Eysenck and Rachman (1965).

> "A nine-year-old boy was referred for treatment of a bee phobia. The phobia, which was intense and interfered with his activities (e.g., playing in the garden) had been present for three years. Although the boy could not remember ever having received a bee sting, he knew of several people who had been stung and/or displayed excessive fear of bees." After a full investigation had elucidated the nature of his fear, a hierarchy of anxiety-provoking situations was constructed. The techniques chosen for generating conditioned inhibition were, in this case, relaxation, social approval and feeding responses. The desensitization began with the patient imagining small photographs of bees while being relaxed. The therapist then went through the following hierarchy — large photographs of bees, colored photographs, dead bee in a bottle at the far end of the room, dead bee in bottle brought gradually closer, dead bee out of the bottle, dead bee on his coat, touching dead bee. Having made considerable progress up to this point, it was decided to combine the imaginary desensitization with real-life desensitization, and the same series of steps was worked through until the boy was capable of holding and playing with several dead bees at a time. The boy made rapid progress, and after eight sessions, both he and his mother reported that he was considerably improved. His mother stated that he was "very much improved . . . he no longer has a physical reaction; he used to go white, sweaty, cold and trembling, and his legs were like jelly. He can play alone in the garden quite comfortably." A one-year follow-up has shown no recurrence of his phobia, and the boy continues to progress well both in school and at home.

Miss A.G., a twenty-four-year-old teacher, complained of an inability to undergo injections of any kind. On those few occasions when she had been unable to avoid them, she had always fainted during or immediately after the injection. Her fear of injections was long standing, dating back to either six or seven years of age. She experienced a moderate physical reaction (trembling and butterflies in the stomach) when asked to imagine a person receiving an injection and ordinarily avoided any talk about injections or related topics (e.g., dental treatment). She also complained of a sexual problem and a fear of using internal sanitary pads. It was considered that the sexual problem was secondary to the fear of injections and of using sanitary pads, and accordingly it was decided to treat these two phobias first. The following hierarchy regarding sanitary pads was constructed: box of Tampax®, an opened pad, holding a pad, holding a pad next to the vagina, seeing someone else using a Tampax, placing a pad at the vaginal entrance, sliding it in slowly, completely inserted, walking about with the pad fully inserted.

At the beginning of the fourth session, after the patient had achieved a degree of skill in relaxing, the first three mild items in the hierarchy (i.e., a box of sanitary pads, an open box of pads, holding a pad) were presented twice each. The patient reported that the images had been slightly disturbing but not very vivid. In the next session, items 3, 4 and 5 of the hierarchy were successfully presented. The remainder of the hierarchy was completed over the next four sessions, by which time the patient had made considerable progress with this fear. She was now able to insert sanitary pads reasonably quickly and with little or no pain.

It was then decided to eliminate the fear of injections, and a hierarchy was constructed. The items in this hierarchy were, in ascending order, seeing a hypodermic syringe, holding a syringe, filling a syringe, seeing a cinema slide of a person receiving an injection, seeing a bull receive an injection, seeing a dog receiving an injection, another person being injected, patient being injected at home, patient being injected in a clinic. The first three items in the hierarchy were then presented twice each. They were visualized vividly, and were not at all disturbing. The remainder of the items in the phobic hierarchy were eliminated during the next five sessions. The patient was then given a practice injection while under relaxation, and this was followed a week later by a normal injection given at a public health clinic. On both occasions she experienced a small measure of unpleasantness but was able to cope on both occasions and showed no signs of fainting or any other unadaptive reaction.

The patient's sexual problem centered around a fear of sexual penetration coupled with a degree of pain experienced during intercourse. With the dissipation of the sexual anxiety and the sanitary-pad fears, a small improvement in sexual responsiveness had been noted to occur spontaneously. This process was enhanced and facilitated by some brief desensitization to sexual situations, and the patient's sexual behaviour was, at the end of the twenty-second session of treatment, notably improved. She was accordingly discharged and seen for follow-ups at two-monthly intervals. At these follow-up interviews she reported that she was substantially improved and felt a great deal better in all respects. All the improvements effected during therapy were maintained for a long time, and when the patient was seen five years after the completion of the treatment, she reported that she had not experienced any recurrence of the phobias. None of her original symptoms had reappeared despite the fact that she had been exposed to stressful conflict situations which had lasted for nearly two years.

Mr. N.R. was a twenty-one-year-old medical student who sought treatment because of intense anxiety about examinations. It became apparent during the two initial interviews that N.R.'s problem was not restricted to a fear of examinations — he also suffered from quite intense social fears of a wide range and type. He was intense, shy, and had great difficulty managing his affairs when they involved other people. His social activities were very restricted.

In the case of N.R. it was then decided to treat the examination phobia and also his fear of people and specific social situations. Three hierarchies were constructed for this patient, the first consisting of a number of examination situations including preparation for the examination, written and oral examinations, important and not-so-important tests, and so forth. The second hierarchy consisted of a number of people who provoked fear reactions in this patient, and he was asked to imagine himself in various situations coming into touch with these people. The third hierarchy consisted of a series of social situations which ordinarily produced fear and avoidance behavior. The three hierarchies were then desensitized in turn, and considerable progress was made. It should be pointed out, however, that because of the social nature of many of this patient's fears, he was also instructed to use an additional technique (assertive training). At the termination of treatment, N.R. was able to cope with examination stresses in a normal manner, had ceased avoiding the people who had formerly frightened him, and was able to mix freely in normal social situations.

It is worth mentioning that the type of treatment described here is prepared and conducted in such a way as to highlight the connections between stimuli (situations) and intense and persistent fear reactions in the patient. "In attempting to analyse neurotic behavior in terms of stimulus and response connections, it is almost invariably found that the response is a relatively pure anxiety response, or at least heavily colored by anxiety. The problem then becomes one of isolating the trigger stimulus and tracing the connection between the stimulus and the anxiety it produces. It also follows that when an analysis of this kind is carried out, many patients will be given the label of *anxiety neurosis,* when viewed from another theoretical standpoint they might well be diagnosed in a different manner" (Eysenck and Rachman, 1965).

Therapists who adhere to other theories and practices have been known to comment that the cases reported by behavior therapists often appear to be, by their standards, straightforward and uncomplicated. In reply, Wolpe has argued that the "simplicity" or "complexity" of neurotic disorders is very often a function of the therapist rather than of the illness itself. He states that unless one is predisposed to analyze neurotic and phobic disorders in terms of stimulus and response relationships, it is indeed very difficult to produce clear-cut descriptions of the particular disorder under consideration.

A behavioristic analysis of a case frequently elaborates straightforward relationships between the trigger stimuli and the anxiety responses, which then give the neurosis a phobia-like appearance. "The distinctive feature of a classical phobia is the presence of clearly ostensible sources of anxiety . . . a behavioristic analysis aims at the liquidation of these sources in every case" (Wolpe, 1958). When viewed in learning-theory terms, anxiety states and phobias, and indeed many other neurotic disorders, are seen to share important characteristics. Consequently, many of the laboratory findings in the field of anxiety and phobias can be applied equally well to various types of neurosis.

Needless to say, desensitization treatment is not always successful. Wolpe and Lazarus (1966) draw attention to three main difficulties which have been found to arise in this type of treatment. They are difficulties of relaxation, misleading or irrelevant hierarchies, and inadequacies of imagery. It should be pointed out, however, that most patients appear to find the treatment acceptable, and that the majority of them do respond favorably in a comparatively short course of treatment.

Difficulties in relaxation can occur for a number of reasons. In some instances it arises because the patient is anxious about some aspect of the relaxation situation itself. Sometimes they are frightened of losing control, or they are so tense that it becomes impossible for them to adhere to the normal practice routine. Another source of difficulty which is sometimes encountered is inaccurate reporting by the patient. On occasions the patient's report of his feelings can mislead the therapist, who then proceeds to present more disturbing hierarchy items in the mistaken belief that the person is sufficiently relaxed to tolerate them.

The problems which arise from the construction of irrelevant or mistaken hierarchies are obvious. Clearly if one is directing the therapeutic effort at the wrong source of fear, or an irrelevant stimulus-response connection, then any expectation of therapeutic improvement is misguided. There is no certain way of avoiding the construction of incorrect hierarchies other than a constant check on the patient's reactions both in the clinic and in his real-life situation. Errors which arise in hierarchy construction can mostly be attributed to a lack of experience on the part of the therapist or to an extremely unusual type of disorder.

Sometimes therapy is hindered or entirely prevented by the patient's inability to project himself into the phobic or anxiety-producing situations. The patient reports either that he is unable to imagine the scene vividly, or more commonly, that the imaginal situation produces no disturbance whatsoever. In these cases the patient reports that the image seems to him to be unrealistic. Where this problem arises it is sometimes necessary to resort to *in vivo* desensitization instead of the more usual imaginal desensitization.

If real-life desensitization is carried out with a proper regard for the importance of using a dampening, antagonistic, response whenever anxiety arises, there is no reason why it should not be successful. In fact, Meyer and Crisp (1966) frequently combine imaginal and real-life desensitization, and their results are apparently as satisfactory as those reported by most other practitioners. Furthermore, in a small experimental study carried out by Cooke (1965), real-life and imaginal desensitization of spider-phobic subjects produced no major differences in outcome.

Two difficulties which are not mentioned by Wolpe and Lazarus, but which are sometimes encountered, are the following. It has been observed in clinical practice that the nature and ranking of hierarchy items tends to fluctuate at times with certain patients. On occasions the therapist is surprised to find that what was initially ranked as a mildly disturbing hierarchy item has (often inexplicably) changed into a moderately or even a severely disturbing stimulus. When inconsistencies of this type emerge, it is necessary to proceed very cautiously and to make repeated checks on the structure and ordering of each hierarchy.

It has also been observed clinically (Agras, 1965) and experimentally (Rachman, 1966) that the reduction of fear which is achieved in a desensitization session is not necessarily permanent and unchanging. In fact, there is good reason to believe that in a large minority of instances some measure of the original fear will reappear at a later time after it has been successfully reduced in intensity. This phenomenon, however, does not present any major practical obstacle, as it has been shown therapeutically and experimentally that the partial reappearance of fear can be managed by further desensitization without any untoward effect of any kind.

Finally, as will be seen in a later chapter on the clinical effectiveness of this form of treatment, the presence of serious depression or extremely high levels of generalized anxiety can quite conceivably interfere with the expected progress of desensitization treatment.

THE RATIONALE OF SYSTEMATIC DESENSITIZATION

Wolpe (1958) argues that the desensitization procedure produces results by *inhibiting* unadaptive anxiety. The presentation of each hierarchy item elicits a small measure of anxiety which is then doused by the antagonistic, relaxation response. This process of reciprocal inhibition is repeated several times for each anxiety-producing item in the hierarchy; each such dampening of the anxiety reaction contributes to the development of *conditioned* inhibition. As the strength of the "negative" habit of *not responding* anxiously (conditioned inhibition) is increased, the intensity of the phobic reaction is diminished.

Relaxation inhibits anxiety because it is an incompatible, antagonistic response. Jacobson (1938) argues that emotional reactions (such as fear) involve increased muscular activity. "The subjective experience of emotion is largely derived from intensive proprioceptive impulses," and muscular *contraction* occurs in all emotional reactions. "Relaxation," says Jacobson, "would seem to be the opposite state."

This view was recently reasserted and elaborated by Gellhorn (1964). He postulates the operation of a "hypothalamic balance" and states that "reciprocal relations exist between the anterior and posterior hypothalamus." These two areas maintain a "see-saw relation" and if one of them is stimulated (goes up), the other is depressed (goes down).

For example, the temperature threshold of the anterior area is raised during noxious stimulation, but decreased during stroking or caressing. Muscle tension is increased by discharges from the posterior region and decreased by discharges from the (parasympathetic) anterior region. Likewise, peripheral stimuli (such as postural changes, relaxation, etc.) can alter the hypothalamic balance. "A reduction or inhibition of proprioceptive impulses through the blocking of the neuromuscular junction reduces sympathetic and increases parasympathetic discharges and also diminishes the state of critical excitation . . . these experiments are believed to represent a physiological model of the mechanism by which abnormal states of emotional tension are alleviated through various forms of 'relaxation' therapy," (Gellhorn, 1964).

Gellhorn's scheme is in many ways an appealing and sensible model, but it is not sufficient in itself to account for the effects of desensitization therapy. As will be shown in the next chapter, the current evidence strongly suggests that relaxation by itself is not the mechanism which produces therapeutic improvements. Rather, it is the combined effect of relaxation and desensitization. Gellhorn's model may help us to comprehend the mode of anxiety suppression, but not, it seems, the reason for the *permanent* reduction of anxiety reactions.

Another interesting possibility was recently proposed by Lader and Wing (1966). In their discussion of morbid anxiety and habituation, they make certain predictions about the effects of desensitization in the management of phobias. Pointing out that the patient is first taught to relax and then subjected to repeated minimal stimulation, they suggest that the treatment effects "be more simply regarded as straightforward habituation carried out when the habituation rate is maximal, i.e., with the patient at as low a level of activity as possible." Their argument is supported by the inverse relationship between level of activity and rate of habituation which emerged from their experimental investigations on patients suffering from morbid anxiety.

They point out that when "the level of activity obtaining at any moment is low, the intrusion of a repetitive, or continuing, stimulus situation has only a brief effect in raising the level of activity, as the ensuing habituation is not only rapid but becomes more rapid as the level of activity drops closer and closer towards the pre-stimulus level."

On the other hand, "if the level of activity is high, habituation is slow, especially at first." If the patient is overactive, then no habituation occurs, and instead, the effect of each successive stimulus is to produce an increase in the level of activity (see the preceding discussion of the Napalkov phenomenon). They describe this process as a vicious circle and point out that such a feedback system constitutes a danger to the organism because it results in excessive excitation of the central nervous system.

This idea may help to account for the Napalkov phenomenon. The likelihood of a person habituating quickly is determined to a considerable extent by his temperamental endowment. People vary along a continuum from slow to rapid habituators. It would be interesting to relate this variation in habituation to other measures of personality and the concepts of introversion and neuroticism (Eysenck, 1967) and the "weak nervous system" postulated by Pavlov (Gray, 1963). In consequence, the rate of habituation of any person, at any particular time, results from two factors: "First, an innate habituation property, and secondly, the level of activity at that time. The very rapid habituator encounters a repetitive or continuing stimulus, his level of activity rises and as he proceeds to adapt, his activity level drops. With a slow habituator, the stimulus raises the activity level and retards still further the already slow rate of habituation."

In regard to the general hypothesis proposed by Lader and Wing, it would appear to provide a satisfactory explanation of what we might call *extinction effects* in neurotic anxiety and phobias.* If this proves to be the case, they will have helped us better to understand the occurrence of spontaneous remission in phobic and other disorders. It seems less likely, however, that their hypothesis can fully account for the effects of systematic desensitization. This is because, as is shown in the next chapter, positive therapeutic effects appear to be the consequence of repeated exposures to minimal quantities of the anxiety-producing stimulus *and* the simultaneous induction of relaxation.

If the psychological data indicated that the probable mechanism underlying these therapeutic changes followed an extinction model, then the Lader-Wing hypothesis might have been generally applicable. However, it is not impossible to tailor the Lader-Wing hypothesis to the experimental and clinical evidence. It will be recalled that they posit a more rapid rate of habituation when a repetitive or continuing stimulus is presented during periods of low activity. If we assume that the effect of relaxation in the desensitization treatment is to pave the way for lowered activity which then permits habituation to the anxiety-producing hierarchy to take place, then the hypothesis can still be maintained.

Another drawback to the Lader-Wing hypothesis is that habituation effects are generally transient. If a prolonged rest interval is provided after habituation has taken place, the response can usually be reevoked. Desensitization treatment, on the other hand, usually produces *enduring* decrements in response strength,

---

*There is, however, an exception to this assessment: The remarkable persistence of many monosymptomatic phobias, observed by Marks and Gelder (1966), is difficult to account for (see p. 18).

and when carried to a successful conclusion, the treatment produces a permanent elimination of the neurotic response.

Lader (1966) has now reported further evidence in support of this hypothesis. On measures of electrodermal activity, it was found that patients with monosymptomatic, specific phobias, (e.g., snakes, insects) showed fewer spontaneous fluctuations and habituated more rapidly than other types of phobic patients (e.g., agoraphobia, social phobias). A positive relation between these autonomic measures and the patient's response to behavior therapy was also observed — rapid habituators responded best.

Other evidence which is consistent with the Lader-Wing hypothesis can be found in two of the experimental studies on desensitization (see Ch. V). Rachman (1966) found that "flooding" his spider-phobic subjects with high fear intensity images did not produce any reduction in their phobias. Similarly, the desensitization of fear-hierarchy items at the top of the list (i.e., the most disturbing ones) appeared to proceed more slowly than was the case with low items (Rachman, 1966b). Both of these observations can be accommodated by the Lader-Wing hypothesis which posits that habituation occurs most readily under conditions of low arousal.

On the other hand, Cooke's (1965) report that *S*'s with high anxiety-scale scores respond well to desensitization treatment may seem to run counter to the hypothesis. In our view, however, this finding is not a serious difficulty. Cooke's subjects were normal, and the relation between clinical, morbid anxiety and a high score on a psychometric scale is very uncertain. Furthermore, Cooke used very few subjects, and a recent attempt to replicate his result was unsuccessful (Teasdale, 1966).

Other clinical observations which are consistent with the Lader-Wing hypothesis can be found in Wolpe's (1958) own work (and elsewhere). Having observed that some patients with pervasive and/or high levels of anxiety, responded poorly to desensitization, he explored the value of a modified Meduna technique in reducing general anxiety. He found that single inhalations of a CO_2 and O_2 mixture often reduced the patient's level of anxiety to a point which then permitted him to employ normal conditioning treatment. For example, Case 10 (Wolpe, 1958, p. 170) made little progress under desensitization treatment "because the patient had a high level of anxiety." The reduction of the patient's phobias (of illness and insanity) was eventually achieved by desensitization, after his general anxiety had been reduced by the CO_2 inhalation.

Recently Slater and Leavy (1966) produced some experimental evidence in support of the claim that the inhalation of a 35 per cent CO_2 – 65 per cent O_2 mixture does in fact reduce the general anxiety level. Another clinical finding which is consistent with the Lader-Wing proposal is the observation that, in some cases, the anxiety hierarchies tend to fluctuate spontaneously. This instability may be accounted for by fluctuations in the patient's level of activity.

Numerous possibilities arise from the Lader-Wing hypothesis. Some of the obvious questions which will need to be investigated include the following.

They suggest that sedating drugs should facilitate the desensitization process. If they are correct in this prediction (and in other respects), then it should also follow that habituation of the GSR (in their experimental situation) should be facilitated by the use of relaxation techniques.

In discussing the relation between habituation and level of arousal, they appear to regard the latter as a more or less enduring state. At the very least, it is assumed to be comparatively constant during the habituation test period. Wolpe's (1958) conception of the mechanism underlying desensitization treatment differs on this point. He postulates that the repeated elicitation of mild anxiety and its repeated inhibition by an antagonistic response (usually relaxation) produces lasting decrements of the anxiety responses. Wolpe's model implies a close temporal connection between anxiety and its inhibitor; the Lader-Wing scheme implies that if the arousal level is low, then habituation (extinction?) can occur under the "cover" of this relatively constant and enduring state – a sort of "psychological hypothermia."

A resolution of these alternatives is desirable for obvious practical and theoretical reasons. For present purposes it is sufficient to point out that confirmation of the Lader-Wing hypothesis would necessitate a change in the desensitization technique. The emphasis would have to move from the present concern with superimposing an antagonistic response whenever anxiety is elicited, to a procedure which can effect a reliable and enduring decrease in arousal level such that desensitization to the hierarchy items can proceed with ease and speed.

There are several ways in which the two alternatives can be investigated and compared. For example, one could ascertain the patient's level of arousal throughout a Wolpeian desensitization session and attempt to relate these observations to measured decreases in fear. Another approach would be to manipulate the temporal relations between the presentation of the hierarchy items and the induction of relaxation, and so on. In our view, however, a direct comparison would be the most fruitful tactic to employ at the present time.

Two matched groups of phobic patients should receive either of the following treatment procedures. The control group should be treated by the orthodox Wolpeian desensitization method. The experimental group of patients should be relaxed at the beginning of each session until the level of arousal is noticeably reduced. Thereafter, the hierarchy items should be presented but no further relaxation instructions must be given. All the treatment sessions in both groups should include physiological recordings.

Incidentally, the investigation adumbrated here is not dissimilar to the research on Brietal desensitization discussed in Chapter VI, and clearly the results obtained with that and other drugs will have a bearing on the two models discussed here.

Chapter V

THE EXPERIMENTAL BASIS OF DESENSITIZATION TREATMENT

Little Miss Muffet
Sat on a tuffet
Eating her curds and whey.
There came a big spider
Who sat down beside her
And frightened Miss Muffet away.

MUCH OF OUR RECENTLY ACQUIRED knowledge about phobias has been obtained from the study of normal subjects who are frightened of spiders, snakes, worms, and so on. Consequently, modern Muffets with miniphobias are much sought after by psychologists.

Some of the most important experimental work on the subject of systematic desensitization was carried out by Lang and Lazovik. In 1963 they reported on the results of an experiment carried out on nonpsychiatric subjects who suffered from an excessive fear of snakes. This pioneer experiment was carefully and elaborately prepared and the experimental design and execution were of high quality. The stringent controls which they applied enhanced the significance of their findings. The aims of the experiment are described by Lazovik and Lang as follows.

1. To evaluate the changes in snake-phobic behavior that occur over time, particularly the effect of repeated exposure to the phobic object.
2. Compare these changes with those that follow systematic desensitization therapy.
3. Determine the changes in behavior that are a direct function of the desensitization process.

They chose to study snake phobias because of their fairly common occurrence (Geer, 1965) and also because of the assumed symbolic sexual significance attributed to snakes (e.g., Brill, 1949;

Hendrick, 1948). Twenty-four subjects participated in the research. They were all college student volunteers and were selected by a combination of interview, questionnaire and direct exposure to nonpoisonous snakes. Only those subjects who rated their fears as intense and whose behavior in the presence of the snake confirmed this subjective report were used in the experiment.

The subjects were divided into two matched groups, an experimental group consisting of thirteen subjects and a control group comprising eleven subjects. The experimental treatment comprised two essential parts: training and desensitization proper. The training procedure consisted of five sessions of forty-five minutes duration, during which an anxiety hierarchy consisting of twenty situations involving snakes was constructed. The subjects were then trained in deep relaxation and taught how to visualize the feared scenes vividly while under hypnosis.

Following this training period, the experimental subjects were given eleven sessions of systematic desensitization during which they were hypnotized and instructed to relax deeply. The anxiety items from the hierarchy were then presented, starting with the least frightening scenes and working up the scale to the most frightening scenes. As the experimental design demanded that each treated subject receive only eleven treatment sessions, some of the subjects were not desensitized to all of the items in the hierarchy.

In order to assess the effectiveness of reality training, half of the experimental subjects were exposed to the snake before treatment on a number of occasions. The control subjects did not participate in desensitization, but they were evaluated at the same time as their opposite numbers in the experimental series and their behavior in the presence of the snake was ascertained at the beginning and the end of the experiment. All of the available subjects were seen and evaluated six months after the completion of therapy.

The authors summarized their results in the following way.

> The results of this present experiment demonstrate that the experimental analogue of desensitization therapy effectively reduces phobic behaviour. Both subjective rating of fear and overt avoidance

> behaviour were modified and these gains were maintained or increased at the six-months follow-up. The results of objective measures were in turn supported by extensive interview material. Close questioning could not persuade any of the experimental subjects that their desire to please the therapist had been a significant factor in their change. Furthermore, in none of these interviews was there any evidence that other symptoms appeared to replace the phobic behaviour. The fact that no significant change was associated with the pre-therapy training argues that hypnosis and general muscle relaxation were not in themselves vehicles of change. Similarly, the basic suggestibility of the subject must be excluded . . . clearly the responsibility for the reduction in the phobic behaviour must be assigned to the desensitization process itself.

Lang and Lazovik also found a very close connection between the degree of improvement and the amount of progress made in the desensitization of hierarchy items within the eleven sessions provided by the experiment. They also make three general points on the basis of their results. First, as has been argued on previous occasions (see Eysenck and Rachman, 1965), it is not necessary to "explore with the subject, the factors contributing to the learning of a phobia or its unconscious meaning in order to eliminate the fear behaviour." Second, they were not able to find any evidence to support the presumed claim that symptom substitution will arise if the symptoms are treated directly. Third, they point out that in reducing phobic behaviour, it is not necessary to alter the basic attitudes, values or personality of the subject.

Lang, Lazovik and Reynolds (1966) recently reported further developments with this experimental procedure. They have now completed a study which included the experimental treatment of twenty-three subjects by systematic desensitization, eleven untreated controls and a further ten subjects who participated in "pseudo-therapy." This last group of subjects is a particularly important addition, as they received the same preliminary training as the desensitization group and participated in the same number of interview sessions.

The major difference was that the pseudo-therapy group was relaxed in the interview sessions but not desensitized — instead the therapist carefully avoided presenting any anxiety-provoking stimuli. The subjects were under the impression that they were being given a form of dynamic or interpretive therapy. The essential difference in the treated and pseudo-therapy groups lay then in the use of systematic desensitization. Consequently any difference in the treatment outcome must be attributed to the use of this behavior-therapy technique.

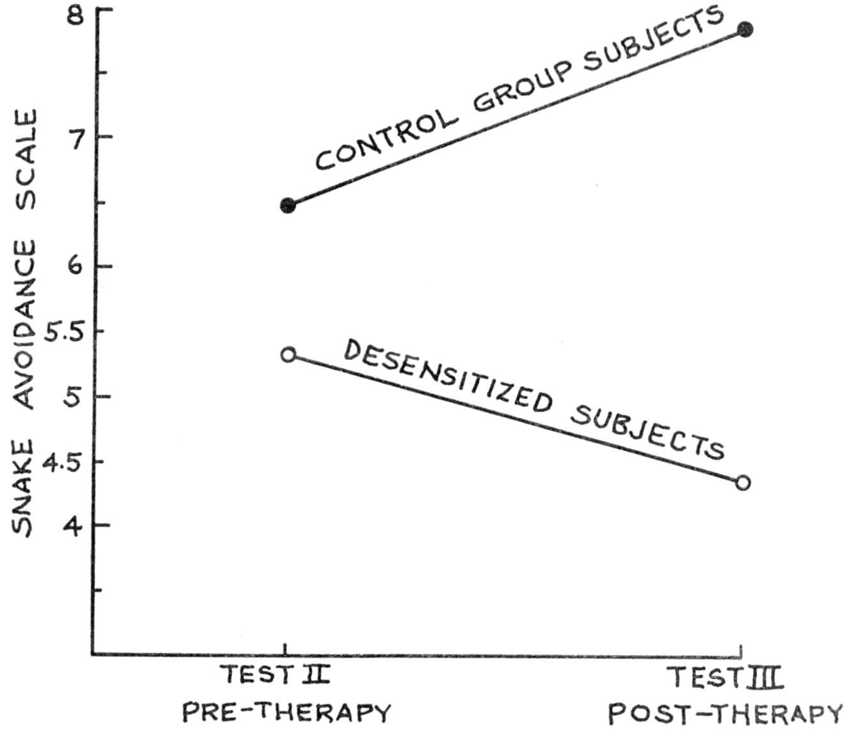

FIGURE 5. The results of an experiment on desensitization. The figure indicates changes in snake-phobic behavior in a group of desensitized subjects and the absence of improvement in the control group subjects. Adapted from Lang and Lazovik (1963).

The results were clear-cut, and indicated that the subjects treated by systematic desensitization showed significant reductions in phobic behavior. The untreated subjects and the subjects who participated in pseudo-therapy showed no improvement whatever.

Among the subsidiary observations made by these research workers, the following are of particular interest. None of the successfully treated subjects showed signs of developing substitute symptoms. Again, it was found to be unnecessary to delve into the presumed basic causes of their fear of snakes. Simply being in a therapeutic relationship with the therapist is not sufficient to effect changes in the phobia. Successful behavior therapy is completely independent of the subject's basic suggestibility (as assessed on the Stanford scale). The systematic desensitization of the specific fear generalizes positively to other fears and an all-round improvement is observed.

Substantially confirmatory results were also reported in an experiment by Paul (1966). He investigated the effectiveness of desensitization in reducing interpersonal performance anxiety (actually, fear of public speaking). Five groups of carefully matched students were randomly allocated to the following groups: (1) systematic desensitization ($n = 15$), (2) insight therapy ($n = 15$), (3) attention placebo ($n = 15$), (4) no-treatment control ($n = 29$), (5) no contact.

Each of the seventy-four students comprising the first four groups was assessed before and after completion of the experiment on three different types of scale. These measures included a number of self-report questionnaires, physiological measures (pulse rate and palmar sweating) and a rating of their behavior in a real-life stress situation (which involved speaking in public).

Five experienced therapists participated in the experiment after having received a brief but intensive training in the desensitization technique. One of the interesting sidelights to emerge from this experiment was the apparent success with which these predominantly interpretive or nondirective therapists acquired the ability to use desensitization treatment.

Each therapist was allotted patients from the three treatment groups (i.e., desensitization, insight, attention-placebo). On the completion of a comparatively short period of treatment (five hours over six weeks), all the subjects, including the nontreatment controls, were retested. The results indicated that the subjects who had received desensitization treatment showed a significantly better response to treatment than any of the other subjects. This superiority was evident on all three types of measurement — subjective report, physiological arousal and reaction to stress. The superiority of the desensitized group was maintained at the six-week follow-up period.

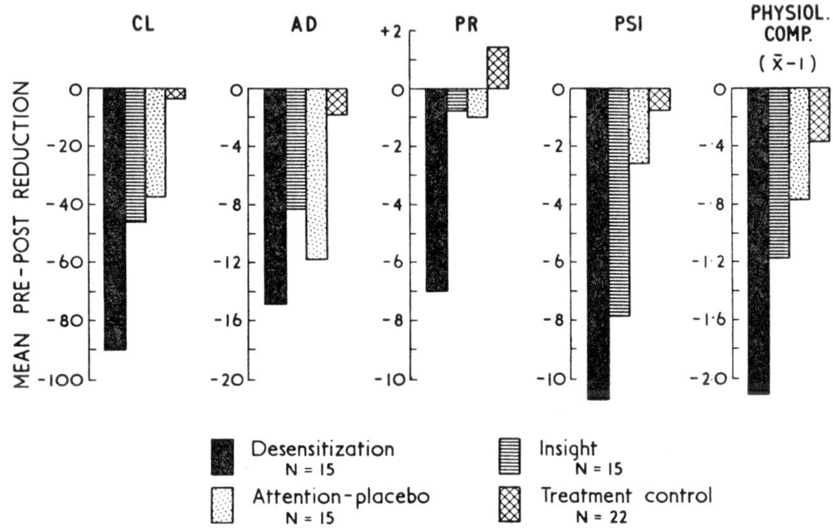

FIGURE 6. Mean reduction in observable manifestations of anxiety (CL), cognitive experience of anxiety (AD), and physiological arousal (PR,PSI) and standardized composite of PR and PSI from pretreatment to post-treatment stress conditions. Reproduced from G. L. Paul (1966).

Like the experiments conducted by Lang and Lazovik, the work of Paul indicates that it is possible to bring about significant reductions in fear, even long-standing fears, by the use of systematic desensitization. It also indicates that fears can be eliminated without any exploration in depth. It would appear then that it is neither insight nor hindsight which is necessary, but rather efficacious techniques for eliminating unadaptive emotional reactions and behavior.

It should be pointed out, however, that this study by Paul is best regarded as an investigation of the effectiveness of desensitization in its own right, and not as a demonstration of the superiority of this technique over other forms of therapy, particularly interpretive or insight treatment. Such a brief period of treatment cannot be regarded as a fair test of "insight therapy," which by general agreement is a procedure requiring a great deal of time to execute.

Paul anticipated this objection by referring to reports of the success of brief psychotherapy and counseling and by pointing out that most patients suffering from anxiety currently receive *brief* therapy. These arguments are of practical importance and are well taken. Nevertheless it seems to be unfair to long-term therapies such as psychoanalysis to refer to the procedure as "insight" treatment; *brief psychotherapy* is perhaps a more accurate description of Paul's procedure. Also, it must be remembered that some measure of improvement was also obtained in the placebo and insight groups. This may well be attributed to the fact that all the subjects continued to attend their normal classes in public speaking.

Finally Paul's use of the term *follow-up* to denote the reassessment carried out six weeks after the completion of the experiment can be misleading. This is not in the ordinary sense a follow-up, but should be regarded more correctly as a post-treatment assessment. Only one of the ten assessment procedures was readministered twice after treatment had been completed. The stability of the changes induced by desensitization therapy is better tested by other studies, such as those carried out by Lang and Lazovik. Nevertheless, the corroborative value of Paul's study is impressive.

In a recent development of this study, Paul and Shannon (1966) demonstrated that systematic desensitization "can be efficiently combined with group discussion and administered in groups without loss of effectiveness in the treatment of interpersonal performance anxiety." Ten chronically anxious students were treated in two groups of five each; nine weekly sessions were given. Significant improvements were obtained at the completion of the group treatment; the ten subjects were shown to be considerably less anxious than the ten untreated control subjects with whom they were compared.

A comparison between the group treatment results with the

individual desensitization treatment results obtained in Paul's (1966) earlier study indicated that "the changes obtained for the group treatment equalled or excelled those obtained for individual treatments on every scale." Kondas (1967) also obtained positive results with group-desensitization treatment of pupils and students with examination anxiety. Comparable groups of subjects treated by autogenic relaxation, by desensitization without relaxation, or left untreated failed to evidence improvements.

A very tightly controlled investigation of the effect of desensitization was recently carried out by Davison (1965). He had two main aims in designing his study. First, he wanted to examine the overall effect of desensitization treatment when compared with a no-treatment control group. Second, he was interested in teasing out the effective elements of desensitization treatment.

He used twenty-eight nonpsychiatric female subjects, all of whom complained of and demonstrated excessive fear of snakes. Subjects were divided into four matched groups on the basis of their behavior in the presence of real snakes. Group No. 1 received desensitization under relaxation, in the usual manner. The second group received relaxation training, but during the treatment sessions, these subjects were given irrelevant images to consider while under deep relaxation. The third group of subjects was given desensitization without either receiving training in relaxation or being relaxed in the actual treatment sessions. The fourth group of subjects received no active treatment, but were merely assessed before and after completion of the experiment.

The subjects in groups 2 and 3 were "yoked" to the systematic desensitization subjects, thereby ensuring that all of the girls who received treatment of any kind received the same number and duration of exposures to imaginary stimuli. The same therapist acted for all the subjects. At the completion of treatment, the retest avoidance exposures showed that the "desensitization under relaxation" group evidenced greater improvements than the other three groups, which did not differ. It was also observed that the subjects who were asked to imagine the anxiety-provoking stimuli without first being relaxed signalled anxiety far more often during treatment sessions than the other subjects.

The importance of this study, apart from providing another demonstration of the undoubted effectiveness of desensitization in eliminating or reducing fears, is that it helps to isolate the mechanisms which produce the reductions in fear. Davison has demonstrated in this experiment that it is neither relaxation alone nor desensitization alone which produces the improvements. Rather it is a combination of desensitization *and* relaxation which reduces fear.

Apart from its practical importance, this experimental result goes some way towards confirming Wolpe's theoretical account of his treatment procedure. One would predict on the basis of his ideas of reciprocal inhibition that neither desensitization nor relaxation would in themselves be adequate procedures for eliminating fear.

A very similar result was also reported by Rachman in 1965. In this study four small groups of spider-phobic, nonpsychiatric subjects were allocated to the following experimental groups: desensitization with relaxation, desensitization without relaxation, relaxation only, no-treatment controls. The purpose of the experiment was "further to explore the effective mechanism contained in the treatment called 'systematic desensitization' based on relaxation."

What are the necessary parts of the treatment procedure? "Three specific questions were framed: Is the treatment more effective than no treatment? Is the treatment more effective than relaxation alone? Is the treatment more effective than desensitization without relaxation?"

The effects of treatment were assessed by subjective reports, avoidance tests and fear estimates. "Marked reductions in fear were obtained only in the desensitization-with-relaxation group, and it was concluded that the combined effects of relaxation and desensitization produce the required changes. Neither relaxation nor desensitization are effective in their own right. The catalytic effect of the two procedures is greater than their separate actions. It means also that the learning process involved is probably conditioned inhibition rather than extinction. This is not meant to imply that extinction is never responsible for the reduction of fear. In the present context however, inhibition is a more effective process."

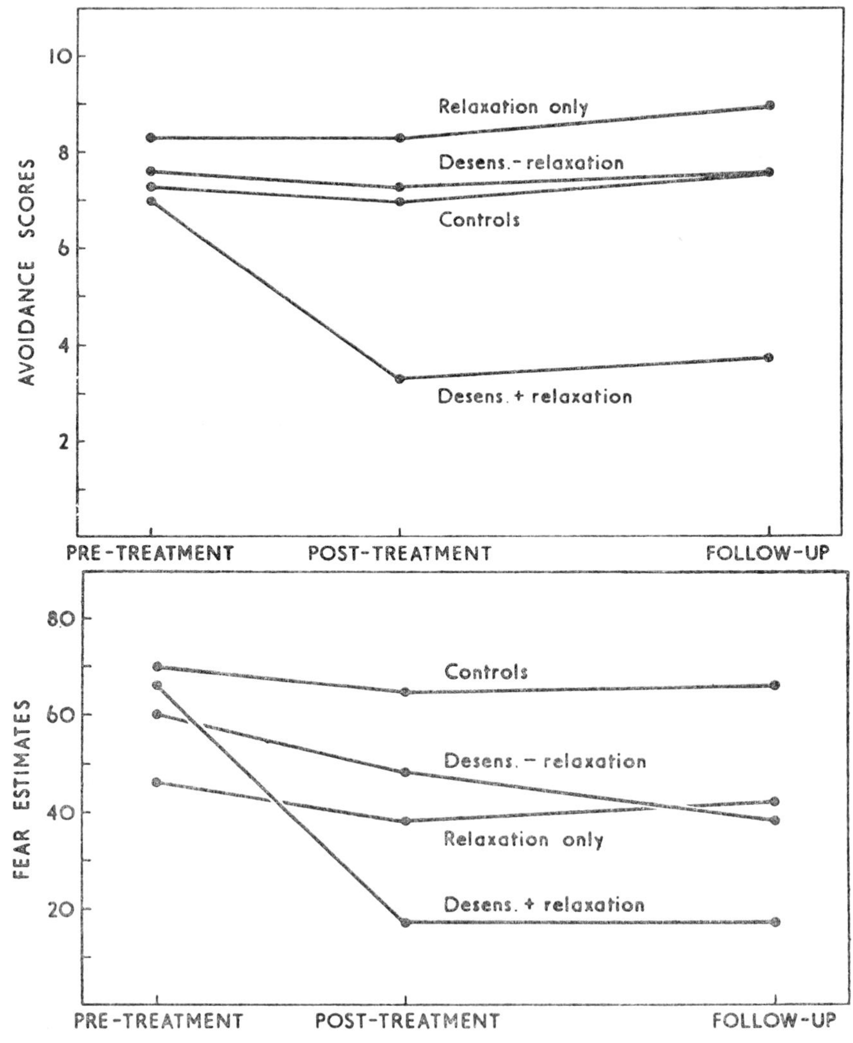

FIGURE 7. A comparison of the results obtained with spider-phobic subjects under four experimental conditions. The subjects who received desensitization under relaxation showed clear improvements on spider-avoidance tests and subjective fear ratings. Reproduced from Rachman (1965).

Like Davison, Paul and Lang and Lazovik, Rachman could adduce no evidence of symptom substitution. Moreover, the improvements in phobic behavior observed at the end of treatment were found to be reassuringly stable over a three-month follow-up period.

The fact that desensitization (i.e., graded and gradual exposures to the fearful stimuli) without relaxation is less effective than the same procedure carried out under relaxation supports Wolpe's conception of the effects of this treatment. He regards reciprocal *inhibition* as the main basis for the reduction and elimination of anxiety.

In a stimulating article on this subject, Lomont (1965) argued that extinction rather than counterconditioning may be the process underlying the observed reductions in fear. In a reexamination of a number of experiments with animals, he could find only two studies in which the introduction of an inhibiting counter-response appeared to produce superior results.

An experiment by Gale, Strumfels and Gale (1966) clearly indicates the superiority of the inhibition technique. Three groups of rats were matched on the basis of their acquisition of a conditioned emotional reaction and then subjected to extinction treatment, inhibition treatment and nontreatment, respectively. The addition of a feeding response during the repeated and progressive introduction of the fear stimulus (inhibition treatment) produced a quicker and greater reduction in fear. As mentioned previously, the evidence from analog studies on human subjects also points to the superiority of the inhibition procedure.

In a recent study, Lomont and Edwards (1966) subjected some of Lomont's theoretical deductions to an experimental test. In particular, they attempted to answer two questions:

"1. Is the efficacy of systematic desensitization due at all to the contiguity of muscular relaxation with anxiety-stimulus visualization?

"2. Can the efficacy of the technique be more satisfactorily explained in terms of reciprocal inhibition than on the basis of extinction?"

The aims of the study are of course similar to those on which Rachman's (1965) investigation was based, and the experimental procedure is also comparable. Two groups of snake-phobic students ($n = 11$ in each group) were treated. The first group received desensitization treatment with relaxation and the second group was given desensitization without relaxation (extinction procedure). On three of the five measures of snake-phobic change, systematic desensitization "produced significantly greater or very nearly significantly greater fear reduction than the extinction procedure," which appeared to be "totally ineffective."

This experimental outcome is consistent with the results reported by Rachman (1965), Davison (1965), and Kondas (1967) in their comparable investigations. At the very least, these four studies now justify the conclusion that reciprocal inhibition produced by relaxation is superior to extinction as a method for reducing fear.

It should be remembered, however, and Lomont's (1965) article demonstrates this lucidly, that extinction procedures can and do effect reductions of fear. The assumed operation of extinction processes is indeed an important feature of the learning-theory view of neurotic disorders proposed by Eysenck and Rachman (1965). Among other things, it is said to be largely responsible for the frequent occurrence of spontaneous remissions of neurotic disturbances. This view is also expressed by Lomont.

Cooke (1966) compared the relative effectiveness of two types of desensitization treatments — imaginal desensitizing *vs.* real-life desensitizing. He employed three groups of nonpsychiatric subjects with excessive fears of rats. Each group consisted of four subjects; their fear reactions were ascertained by avoidance tests in the usual manner (see Lang and Lazovik, 1963; Paul, 1966). The first group was relaxed and then exposed in a graded and gradual manner to real rats, while the second group was relaxed and desensitized to similar items in imagination only. The third group consisted of a no-treatment control.

Cooke found no overall difference between the two types of treatment, both of which produced significant decreases in fear. He found, however, that highly anxious subjects showed more fear reduction when treated in the Wolpeian fashion with imaginal stimuli. This difference in the response to treatment of slightly and highly anxious subjects is of some interest because of the clinical reports, which have suggested that anxious patients do not respond to behavior therapy as well as less-anxious patients (see Wolpe, Salter and Reyna, 1965; Lazarus, 1963; Marks and Gelder, 1966).

In a sense, Cooke's results run counter to these clinical findings which all tend to show that anxious subjects respond more slowly to behavior therapy. Clearly this is a point which needs further investigation, especially as a small-scale replication study by Teasdale (1966) with six spider-phobic subjects failed to produce different results in the high- and low-anxious groups. Paul (1966) was also unable to find results which support Cooke's conclusion. Some other findings which emerge from Cooke's study and are of interest include the following: No symptom substitution was observed nor were any increases in anxiety noted after treatment. Cooke also remarks on the consistency and reliability of the avoidance test scores and the subjective fear estimates.

Two other aspects of desensitization treatment which have received recent attention are the distribution of treatment sessions and the speed of generalization from imaginal desensitization to real-life behavior. Ramsay *et al.* (1966) compared the effectiveness of massed and spaced treatment sessions. Twenty nonpsychiatric subjects with fear of various animals were given desensitization treatment under conditions of massed and spaced practice. In the spaced practice condition, each subject was given four fear-hierarchy stimuli to imagine in a twenty-minute period. Four such treatment sessions were given. For the massed practice group, each treatment session contained eight items, and the session lasted for forty minutes. Two of these prolonged sessions were administered. Thus the subjects in the two groups received the same amount of time in treatment and the same number of item presentations.

The results showed a highly significant drop in fear due to the treatment, and the learned reductions in fear were more efficiently induced under the distributed practice condition. Ramsay *et al.* comment in passing on the ease with which the experimental therapists (with no previous experience of desensitization) acquired the necessary skill in successfully administering the treatment.

Rachman (1966) described an exploratory investigation into the speed of generalization from desensitization treatment conditions to real-life situations. The two main aims of the study were to "search for time lags and to pin down the time at which the generalization occurs." A subsidiary purpose in carrying out the investigation was to see if it could throw any light on the occurrence of relapse after desensitization treatment.

The basic design of the study consisted of the following steps. The subject was exposed to an anxiety-provoking stimulus involving spiders and asked to estimate the degree of fear which developed. This pretreatment assessment was immediately followed by desensitization treatment usually lasting approximately fifteen minutes. In every case the subject was desensitized to an imaginal representation of the identical stimulus used in the pretreatment avoidance test. Immediately after the completion of the desensitization the subject was reexposed to the original stimulus *in vivo*. This avoidance test was then repeated twenty-four hours later, and once more, three days or one week later.

Measurements of the subject's reaction to the phobic stimulus were thus obtained on four occasions: immediately pretreatment, immediately post-treatment, twenty-four hours later and one week later. It was found that the reductions in fear transfer from the original desensitization session almost immediately. Spontaneous recovery of some degree of fear (i.e., relapse) occurred in slightly less than 50 per cent of the occasions tested. The last finding is consistent with the clinical observations reported by Agras (1965). It is to be hoped that the design used in this experiment will be repeated and extended with a view to investigating the possible causes of clinical relapse. It is also of interest in demonstrating not only the frequency with which generalization does occur, but also, fairly precisely, when such transfer takes place.

A slightly atypical experiment was carried out by Lazarus in 1961. It affords some evidence in support of the effectiveness of

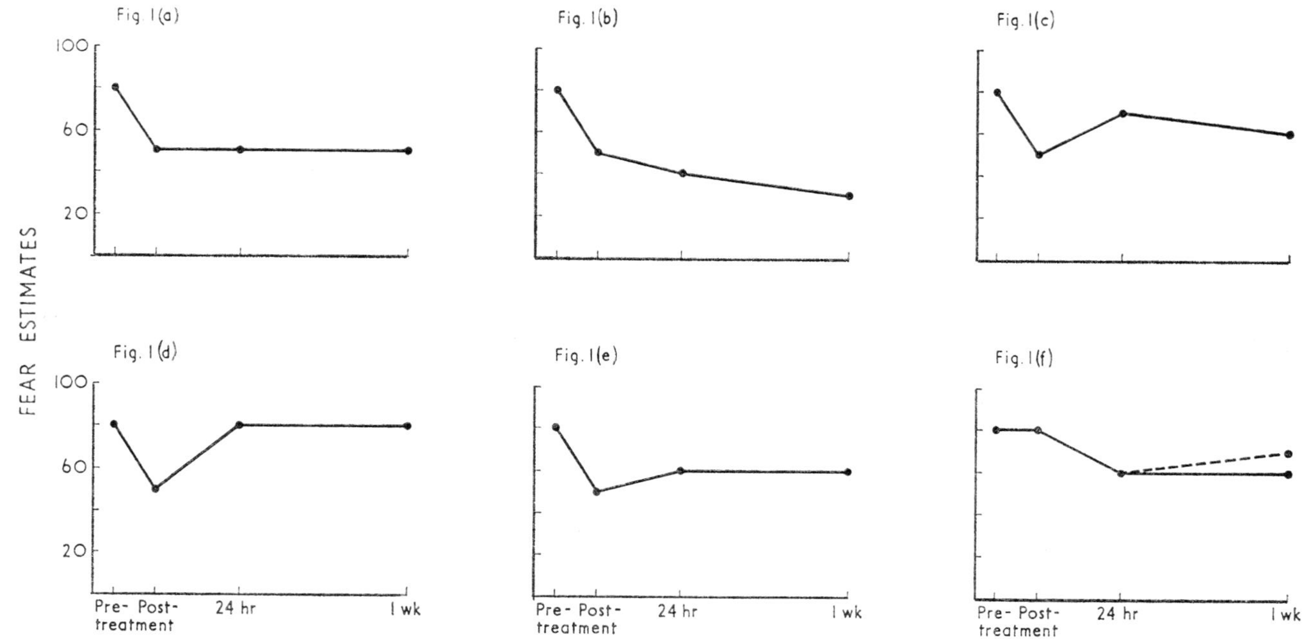

FIGURE 8. Theoretically, a large variety of responses to desensitization sessions can be expected. In practice, the above six patterns of reaction were the only ones to appear with any frequency. Types 1 (a), 1 (b) and 1 (c) were the most common, and it was noted that the reduction of fear which was achieved in imaginal desensitization transferred to the real situation *immediately* in 82 per cent of the observations. Reproduced from Rachman (1966a).

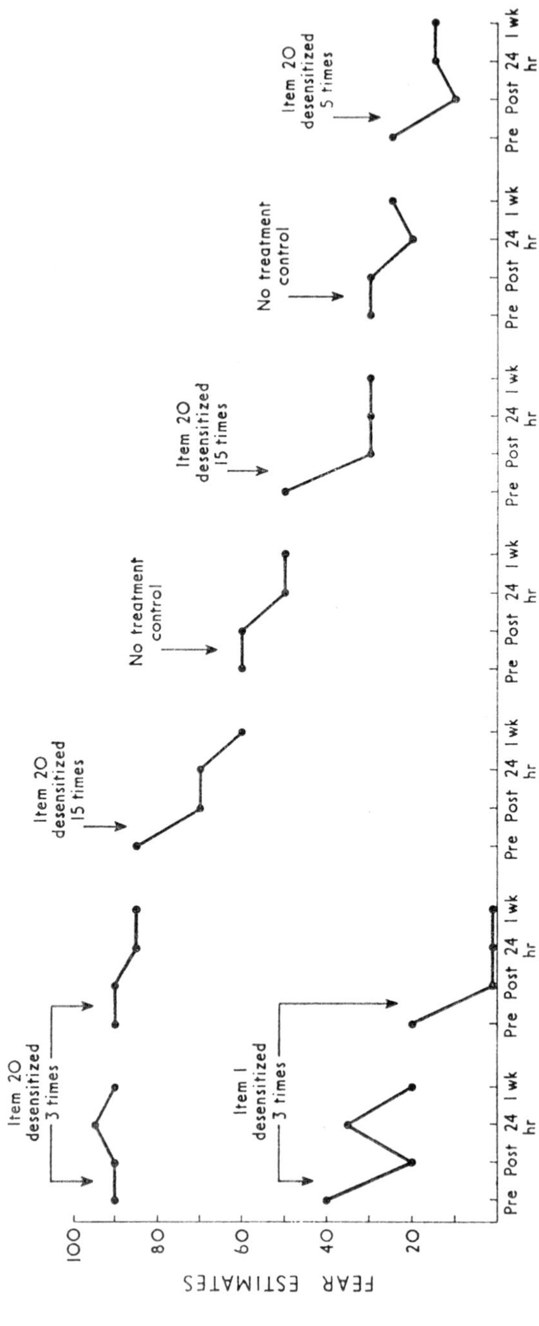

FIGURE 9. The varied effects produced by inhibition and extinction can be illustrated in the session-by-session treatment of the most disturbing item (No. 20) encountered in one subject's hierarchy. In each of the first two attempts, the imaginal stimulus (handling a live spider) was presented three times, as usual. Practically no fear reduction was obtained. In the next session, the stimulus was presented fifteen times and was followed by a decrease in fear. A no-treatment check was then given at the next session. No immediate change occurred, but a slight gain was observed twenty-four hours later. At the next session, fifteen desensitization trials were given and a substantial improvement was immediately noted. A second no-treatment check again produced slight gains at followup.

For purposes of comparison, Figure 9 also includes the treatment progress of the lowest item (No. 1) in this subject's hierarchy (a small, dead spider ten yards away). This stimulus was desensitized easily and rapidly. In all, our experiences with the concentrated study of response to treatment were consistent with Wolpe's (1963) model of proximation phobias and Agras's (1965) clinical findings. Phobias in which the anxiety increases with proximity to the feared object, require few desensitization trials to eliminate the lowest hierarchy items. As the fear object is approached, however, an increasing number of practice trials is required (Eysenck and Rachman, 1965). Reproduced from Rachman (1966b).

systematic desensitization. This study was unusual (1) in that the treatment was carried out in groups rather than in individual treatment sessions, and (2) because of the heterogeniety of the sample used. The group desensitization technique had never been used before, so Lazarus' study to a large extent was exploratory rather than confirmatory. The results were nevertheless favorable to the desensitization approach and have now received a measure of support from the experiment recently reported by Paul and Shannon (1966).

Altogether Lazarus treated seventeen control subjects and eighteen experimental subjects. The sample consisted of four types of patients. These were eleven acrophobics, fifteen claustrophobics, five cases of impotence and four mixed disorders. The experimental subjects were treated in four separate groups, varying in size from two to five subjects; the control subjects were treated in groups of not less than three subjects at a time.

The experimental subjects were trained in relaxation and were given desensitization training, and eventually, desensitization treatment. The first control group was given group interpretive therapy, and the second control group (consisting of eight patients), received interpretive therapy and relaxation. Although the subjects treated by Lazarus were not drawn from a psychiatric population, they were nevertheless severely limited in their social relationships and general psychological adjustment because of their complaints.

Before commencing treatment each subject was interviewed and given psychometric tests, and where possible, was observed in a real-life fear situation. The assessment of the treatment effect was carried out by interview method and also by further excursion into the relevant feared situation. The results showed that a high degree of success was obtained with the group desensitization method, whereas those patients who received interpretive treatment did not show any recoveries.

Of the eight patients treated by group interpretive therapy and relaxation, only two recovered. Follow-up studies were conducted on all the patients who had shown any sign of recovery. The follow-ups were carried out by means of a questionnaire, and

TABLE III
EXPERIMENT ON DESENSITIZATION

Patients	*Treated by Desensitization*	*Recovered*	*Treated by Interpretation*	*Recovered*	*Interpretation and Relaxation*	*Recovered*
Acrophobics	5	4	3	0	3	1
Claustroprobics	7	4	3	0	3	1
Impotence	2	2	3	0	–	–
Mixed	4	3	–	–	–	–
	18	13	9	0	8	2

Adapted from Lazarus (1961), *Journal of Abnormal and Social Psychology.*

any patient who revealed even a slight phobic recurrence was considered to have relapsed.

Although Lazarus paid attention to the question of possible symptom substitution, no evidence of this phenomenon was encountered. Lazarus summarized his results in this way: "Group desensitization was applied to eighteen patients, out of whom thirteen initially recovered and three subsequently relapsed. Group interpretation was applied to nine patients. There were no recoveries in this group. Group interpretation plus relaxation was applied to eight patients, of whom two recovered and one subsequently relapsed. The fifteen patients who had not benefitted from the interpretive procedures were then treated by group desensitization. There were ten recoveries, of whom two subsequently relapsed."

Of the eighteen subjects who were treated by group desensitization, thirteen recovered in a mean of 20.4 sessions. The fifteen patients who were not symptom-free after undergoing interpretive group therapy and who were treated by desensitization showed a 66 per cent recovery rate after a mean of only 10.1 sessions. Lazarus suggests that the fact that these patients recovered in a shorter time than the original experimental subjects indicates they may have received some form of nonspecific benefit from either the relaxation training or from the relaxation training in association with the interpretive therapy. Unfortunately, Lazarus's results cannot be accepted without reserve because the experimental design contained some weaknesses. The possibility that rater contamination and experimenter bias distorted the results cannot be ruled out, because both the treatment and the assessments were carried out by Lazarus himself.

In an experiment on a small group of asthmatic patients who acted as their own controls, Moore (1965) obtained a greater degree of improvement with desensitization treatment than that recorded when the patient received either relaxation or relaxation and suggestion. An interesting aspect of the treatment outcome in this study was that when the *S*'s were merely relaxed, their subjective reports suggested some improvements in their condition, whereas the physiological measurements (respiratory flow) recorded little change. The results revealed significant improvements after systematic desensitization, apparently attributable to the desensitization procedure. In the case of this procedure, subjective reports and physiological tests improved together. For this reason and because of the intrinsic clinical interest of this study, replications and extensions of this experiment would be extremely useful.

The present state of the experimental evidence on desensitization permits the following conclusions. Desensitization therapy effectively reduces phobic behavior. The elimination of phobic behavior is analogous to the elimination of other responses from the subject's repertoire. It is not necessary to ascertain the origin of the phobia in order to eliminate it. Neither is it necessary to change the subject's basic attitudes or to modify his personality. The elimination of a phobia is not followed by symptom substitution. The response to treatment is not related to suggestibility.

Relaxation or hypnosis alone do not reduce the phobia. Relaxation and hypnosis accompanied by pseudotherapeutic interviews do not reduce the phobia. The establishment of a therapeutic relationship with the patient does not of itself reduce the phobia. Desensitization administered in the absence of relaxation appears to be less effective than systematic desensitization treatment. Interpretive therapy combined with relaxation does not reduce phobic behavior. A limited number of observations raise the possibility that reductions in fears which are produced by desensitization occur almost immediately; in a large minority of instances, a proportion of the fear-reduction accomplished in experimental treatment sessions reappears within twenty-four hours.

Although some of these conclusions are tentative (the last two in particular), as a body they constitute a very important advance in our ability to reduce phobias. It is clear nevertheless that there is a great deal which still needs to be investigated and understood. Perhaps the most immediate need is for further experimental studies which attempt to apply these findings to psychiatric patients. While it is true that the clinical reports which have been published to date are, with some exceptions, consistent with the experimental evidence discussed in this paper, there remains a need for careful experimental investigation of the clinical application of desensitization. The recent study reported by Marks and Gelder (1966), is an example of the type of application which is required.

The bulk of the work which has been reported so far has of course been carried out on phobic subjects. There is therefore a need for further investigation of both psychiatric and nonpsychiatric subjects who suffer from complaints other than excessive fears or phobias. Clearly it is necessary to find other psychiatric and nonpsychiatric analogies on which to carry out similar experiments to those already described. One such example is the study carried out by Moore (1965) on asthmatic patients. From an experimental point of view the full range of applicability of desensitization treatment remains to be explored.

One of the specific problems which will have to be reexamined in clinical experiments is the role of anxiety in facilitating or impeding the progress of desensitization treatment. The clinical reports tend on the whole to indicate that the presence of high anxiety impedes or entirely prevents the progress of desensitization treatment (Eysenck and Rachman, 1965). On the other hand, the experiment reported by Cooke suggests that in certain instances at least, the presence of high anxiety might be associated with a speedy response to desensitization.

Closely allied to this problem is the question of the role of depression in desensitization treatment. Several clinical reports (e.g., Hain, Butcher and Stevenson, 1966; Meyer and Crisp, 1966) point out that the presence of depression in psychiatric patients tends to interfere, often quite seriously, with desensitization treatment.

The comparative effectiveness of different therapists is another matter which needs to be examined. In the main, the results available from the experiments in which this variable has featured tend to suggest that intertherapist differences are of minor significance, at least where nonpsychiatric phobic subjects are concerned. It may well be, however, that in the management of severely disturbed patients the ability (or personality ?) of the therapist is of some significance. It must be pointed out, however, that there have been some surprising indications from the experiments on nonpsychiatric subjects suggesting that it is possible to bring about the reduction or elimination of excessive fears with comparatively little training in the desensitization procedure.

Needless to say, the management of psychiatric patients would by its very nature require more prolonged training and experience. In their retrospective analysis of the effects of behavior therapy in general, Marks and Gelder (1964) adduced some evidence to indicate that clinical experience was an important factor in determining the outcome of such treatment. On the technical side, two aspects of the desensitization procedure which would bear further examination are the optimum number and duration of scene presentations during the actual treatment sessions. Another possibility which has not received the attention which one might have expected is the use of drugs to facilitate the treatment procedure (see Wolpe, 1958; Wolpe and Lazarus, 1966; Eysenck and Rachman, 1965).

On the technical side, it is becoming increasingly important to refine and extend the present methods of assessing therapeutic changes. The inclusion of physiological measures is an obvious step, but unfortunately, is still replete with technical difficulties.

Finally, two theoretical advances are worth noting. When behavior therapy was first introduced, numerous objections were raised, particularly in psychoanalytic circles. Two of the most serious and widely expressed criticisms were these. First, it was argued that the tendency of behavior therapists to treat manifest neurotic behavior would, if successful, lead to symptom substitution. That is to say, the patient would develop new and possibly even worse symptoms if the so-called defensive reactions were removed by the behavior therapist. This phenomenon of symptom substitution has, in this event, proved to be of minimal importance, and occurs very rarely. In none of the experiments described above was symptom substitution observed, even though it was in almost all cases carefully sought. In the clinical reports also, the occurrence of symptom substitution is rare (Rachman, 1965).

A second objection which was raised was that it is impossible to bring about the reduction or elimination of neurotic symptoms and behavior unless one first eliminated the presumed basic cause of the illness. It was said that behavior therapy could not succeed because it was directing its attention to the wrong idea. This objection, too, has now been firmly eliminated. In the experimental investigations and the clinical reports there is overwhelming evidence that substantial improvements in neurotic behavior can be obtained by systematic desensitization (and other methods of behavior therapy), even when little or no attention is paid to the possible or presumed underlying causes of the illness.

The predictions inherent in these two objections (i.e., symptom substitution and "basic causes") have not been borne out by the experimental investigations described in this chapter. As a consequence, it has become necessary to go through the uncomfortable process of rearranging one's prejudices.

Chapter VI

CLINICAL RESULTS

THE CLINICAL effectiveness of behavior therapy (and desensitization in particular) is attested to by two types of evidence: individual case histories and field trials. A large number of illustrative case histories is now available, and many of them have been conveniently assembled and reproduced in three or four texts. Descriptions of the clinical method are contained in *Behavior Therapy and the Neuroses,* edited by H. J. Eysenck; *Causes and Cures of Neuroses,* by Eysenck and Rachman; *Psychotherapy by Reciprocal Inhibition,* by Wolpe; *Case Studies in Behaviour Modification,* by Ullmann and Krasner. Cases of unusual interest or particular didactic value are also published in the journal, *Behavior Research and Therapy.*

The first major report on the clinical effectiveness of desensitization and other methods of behavior therapy was provided by Wolpe in 1958. He described the results obtained in the treatment of 210 neurotic patients. Wolpe accepted every patient referred provided that the diagnosis of neurosis had been confirmed. The composition of the sample is adequately described, and it is clear that the majority of his patients were suffering from anxiety states of one type or another. The patients suffering from anxiety were not, however, subdivided into phobics and related conditions, so that it is not possible to provide an accurate estimate of the degree of success which was obtained with specifically phobic disorders. However, 135 of the 210 patients reported in this publication were described as being anxiety neurotics; an examination of the cases in detail makes it fairly clear that many of them were in fact complaining of phobic symptoms of one variety or another.

Wolpe assessed the effectiveness of therapy in terms of five criteria: symptomatic improvement, increased productiveness, improved adjustment and pleasure in sex, improved interpersonal relationships, and the ability to deal with reasonable reality stresses. Each patient was classified in terms of these criteria into one of five categories: apparently cured, much improved, moderately improved, slightly improved, and unimproved. Of the 210 patients treated, approximately 90 per cent were apparently cured or much improved after treatment.

This exceptionally successful result must be regarded with a measure of reserve because of the incomplete nature of the follow-up investigations. It was impossible, for practical reasons, to arrange long-term follow-ups for the majority of these patients, and it seems probable in view of more recent evidence that a proportion of them did not maintain their initial improvements. Another possible source of inflation in this figure can be traced to Wolpe's exclusion from the final assessment of those patients who had not completed a minimum of fifteen treatment sessions. This is an unusually stringent criterion, and one which most of the later clinicians have not used.

This report by Wolpe was the first major account of the systematic attempt to apply principles of learning theory to the treatment of neurotic disturbances. As a pioneering effort, it cannot of course be expected to provide a full answer to the problem of psychotherapy. It is true, nevertheless (and this can be said with increasing confidence, in view of more recent evidence), that the therapy and general approach developed by Wolpe constitutes a clear advance in our ability to treat neurotic disturbances and phobias in particular.

Wolpe's work is attractive for a number of reasons, in addition to the encouraging therapeutic outcome which he obtained. In the first place, it is based on sound psychological principles and was developed in a systematic and logical manner from existing theoretical notions and specially devised experiments. It has the further advantage of being stated and described in such a manner as to permit careful experimental investigation of both the assumptions and actual procedures involved.

In 1963, Lazarus reported on the treatment of 408 patients. These neurotic patients were treated on the lines proposed by Wolpe and were assessed in similar manner. Lazarus was able to obtain significant improvement in 321 of his patients, that is, 78 per cent. He then went on to carry out a detailed analysis of the results obtained with 126 patients who were suffering from what he describes as "severe neurosis." This subanalysis was carried out in an attempt to clarify the position in regard to the effectiveness of behavior therapy with more complex and severe disorders.

Lazarus discovered that the recovery rate for severe cases was only 62 per cent. This figure is of course lower than that obtained in the total series and also lower than that obtained by Wolpe in his major report. The suggestion arising from this subanalysis is that while behavior therapy is probably effective in treating complex neurotic disorders, it may well prove to be more effective in treating simple disorders. Another difference which might account for the reduced improvement rate in Lazarus' group is the fact that each of the 126 severely neurotic patients was followed up for a mean duration of two years.

Other clinical reports have been provided by Hussein (1962), Burnett and Ryan (1965), and by Schmidt *et al.* (1965). As these three clinical reports all described variations on conventional behavior therapy, and because they dealt with a conglomeration of different types of patient, they will not be discussed in any detail here. It is sufficient to say that the success rates varied between 60 per cent and 95 per cent and that the suggestion emerged from the paper by Schmidt *et al.* that patients who had chronic and complicated disorders tended on the whole to do less well than those patients who were less severely ill.

Humphery (1966) recently reported a comparison trial between behavior therapy and psychotherapy in treating neurotic disorders in children. Both methods produced successful results, but behavior therapy was slightly more effective and was significantly quicker than psychotherapy. The long-term results from behavior therapy were found to be superior.

Cooper (1963) reported a retrospective study on the effects of behavior therapy. He carried out a follow-up study of thirty patients who had received various types of behavior therapy at the Maudsley Hospital between 1954 and 1960. Cooper attempted to construct a retrospective control group by matching them with another thirty patients who had been treated at approximately the same time. In fact, he was able to extract only sixteen matched controls from hospital records.

The progress of these matched pairs of patients (ten phobics, four obsessionals, one stammerer and one case of writer's cramp) was then estimated by two independent assessors. Retrospective assessments were made of their progress at the end of treatment, one month, and one year after treatment. Cooper stated that the "only striking finding is at the end of treatment for the 10 phobic patients, 9 of whom showed definite improvement in the symptom treatment compared to only 5 of the control cases." The superior improvement observed in the phobic patients was not apparent at the follow-up assessment, however. Cooper also pointed out that none of the patients had developed substitute symptoms.

Unfortunately, the value of Cooper's study is undermined by several factors. The selection of patients was not properly randomized, as the matching was carried out retrospectively, and as Cooper himself points out, "in some of these cases, behaviour therapy suffered the fate of all new forms of treatment and was tried as a last resort, and some cases were taken on as much experimentally as therapeutically. This was particularly so in obsessional patients. . . ."

Some of the treatment was carried out by students, or by psychologists who had no previous experience of behavior therapy (many of the control patients were treated by trainee psychiatrists.) Thirdly, Cooper provides few details about the nature of the behavior therapy used. His statement that the phobic patients were treated by Wolpe's methods of reciprocal inhibition and desensitization is misleading. In fact, fewer than twenty of the patients in the matched group of therapy cases were treated by the method which Wolpe used in practically all his phobic cases, namely desensitization based on relaxation. Consequently, Cooper's comparison of the results with those reported by Wolpe appears to be unjustified.

Cooper failed to indicate in a clear manner that he was in fact comparing different types of behavior therapy. Moreover, he was comparing different types of patients — many of the

Maudsley group were people who required in-patient hospital care. The great majority of Wolpe's patients were treated on an out-patient basis. A further drawback to Cooper's study was the fact that the assessors worked solely from the case notes and did not interview any of the patients in either the treatment or the control groups. Cooper himself interviewed fourteen of the thirty behavior-therapy patients and none of the controls. For these reasons Cooper's conclusions cannot be accepted at face value.

In an extension of Cooper's study, Marks, Gelder and Cooper (1965) arrived at a similar conclusion when they examined an additional thirty-seven patients treated at the Maudsley Hospital. They claimed that in none of the treatment groups was behavior therapy less effective than other methods of treatment, and that *in the phobias* it was more effective. The development of fresh symptoms after successful behavioral treatment was not a hazard.

Behavior therapy can be effective in severe chronic cases where other methods have been tried and failed, and in some conditions (i.e., monosymptomatic phobias), it may even be the first consideration for treatment. The finding that severe chronic patients do not respond as successfully to behavior therapy as do other types of neurotic patients has in fact received further support in a prospective study which was recently completed.

Gelder and Marks (1966) described a control trial of behavior therapy with twenty severe agoraphobic patients. These patients were carefully matched and placed into either the treatment or control group. The therapy which was administered consisted of graded retraining in real-life situations together with Wolpe's technique of desensitization in imagination. The control treatment was based on brief "re-educative psychotherapy," and both types of treatment were given three times weekly.

In each group seven out of the ten patients improved symptomatically. In both instances, however, the patients were left with much residual disability. This disappointing result appears to have resulted from the fact that the patients concerned were severely ill. The mean duration of the agoraphobic illness was more than seven years, and all the patients were deemed to require in-patient care. As has already been shown in other studies, severely ill patients do not respond as well to behavior therapy as those with less-incapacitating disorders.

Closer inspection of the results indicate, however, that the patients who were treated by behavior therapy had improved slightly more (but not statistically so) than the other group. Moreover, the behavior-therapy group showed "greater improvement in work capacity . . . at the end of treatment." A similar finding was reported by Hain and others (1966).

That the relatively poor results obtained in this control trial can best be attributed to the severity of the illness affecting these patients gained some support from another study reported by Gelder, Marks and Wolff (1967). They reported that a less-satisfactory response to treatment was found in severe agoraphobics than among moderately disturbed (out-patient) phobics.

Although Gelder and Marks did not provide the mean number of sessions of treatment given to the severe agoraphobics, it is apparent from the duration of the treatment (given approximately three times a week) that these patients required considerably more treatment than those described either by Lazarus (1965) or by Meyer and Crisp (1966) or by Hain, Butcher and Stevenson, (1966). The suggestion made by Gelder and Marks that the slightly better outcome for patients who received behavior therapy can be accounted for by the longer duration of treatment is not entirely consistent with the observations reported by Hain and others, who found that there was no correlation in their group of patients, between duration of treatment and therapeutic outcome. Wolpe (1964) himself, however, reported that sixty-five patients with complex neuroses needed an average of 54.8 treatment sessions, whereas twenty-one patients with simple neuroses only required an average of 14.9 sessions.

As in every study on the subject, both clinical and experimental, Gelder and Marks could find no evidence that symptom substitution constitutes a problem. They also emphasize, however, the difficulty encountered in selecting patients for behavior therapy.

These psychiatrists recently added another field trial to their valuable investigations. Gelder, Marks and Wolff (1967) carried out a controlled enquiry into the comparative effectiveness of desensitization, individual psychotherapy or group psychotherapy in the treatment of phobic states. Forty-two moderately disturbed phobic patients were treated on an out-patient basis by one of these three methods. The patient groups were extremely carefully matched and consisted of the following cases: desensitization group — eight agoraphobics, four social phobics, four with specific phobias; group therapy — seven agoraphobics, three social phobias, six specific phobias; individual psychotherapy — seven agoraphobics, three social phobias. They summed up their major findings in this way:

> All raters agreed that, of the three treatments, desensitization produced more patients whose symptoms improved at the end of treatment and follow-up.
>
> Symptoms, especially the presenting phobias, improved faster with desensitization than with psychotherapy. After 6 months, desensitization patients had changed more significantly than others, but this difference diminished later, as the patients in psychotherapy went on improving slowly. Only two patients lost their symptoms completely, both with desensitization. At follow-up the degree of improvement still tended to be greater in those who had been treated with desensitization, but the difference was no longer statistically significant.
>
> Ratings of social adjustment were less sensitive and reliable than symptom ratings; however, greater and more rapid improvement occurred in work and leisure adjustment with desensitization . . . (pp. 71-72). The number of patients whose phobias "were rated much improved by two of three raters at the final rating were: desensitization 9/16; group therapy 2/16; individual therapy 3/10 (p. 60).

In assessing these results (see Figs. 10 and 11), it is important to note that the desensitization group was treated weekly for about nine months and then reassessed nine months later. The patients in group therapy received eighteen months of treatment, and their results do not include a follow-up. The patients who received individual therapy were treated for a year and reassessed six months later. Gelder *et al.* (1967), commenting on their results, occasionally fail to take these differences fully into account.

Although the groups were extremely well matched in particulars, it is a pity that only ten patients were included in the individual therapy group. Perhaps the main weakness in this study is the crudity of the assessment measures (mostly five-point rating scales), but this is a difficulty with which all research workers can sympathize.

In examining the outcome of this trial, it is also worth remembering that many of the subsidiary measures (e.g., of obsessions and also of the therapist's rating of depression — see Fig. 10) deal with minor problems, and it is no surprise therefore that the three treatment groups rarely differ in these respects. Neither desensitization nor psychotherapy can produce superior results with subsidiary problems which are slight to begin with — simply, there is little room for change.

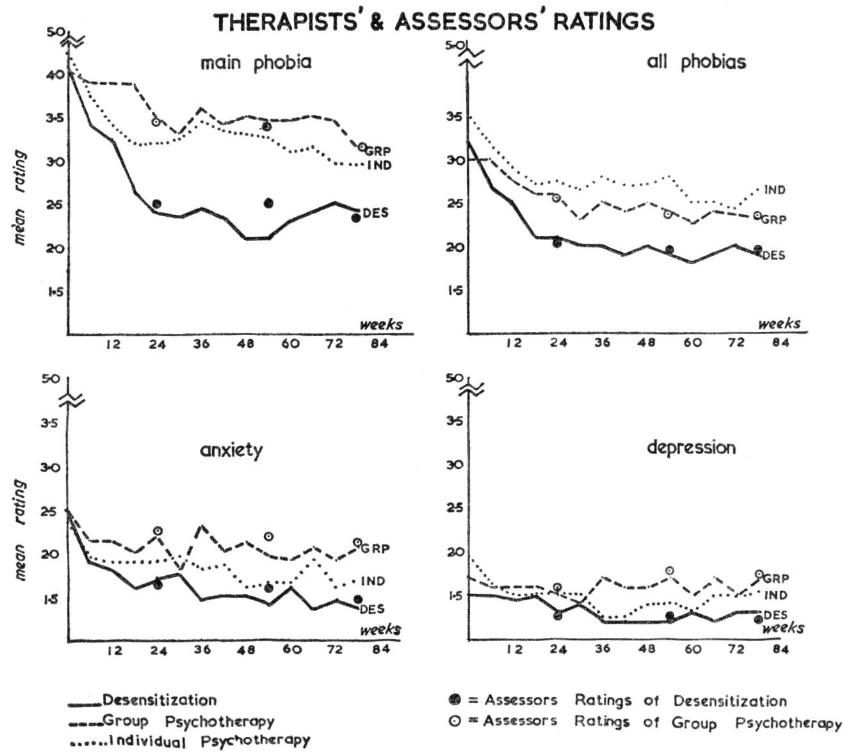

FIGURE 10. Mean psychiatric ratings (average of therapists and assessors ratings) of four symptoms in patients receiving desensitization, individual psychotherapy and group psychotherapy. Reproduced from Gelder, Marks and Wolff (1967).

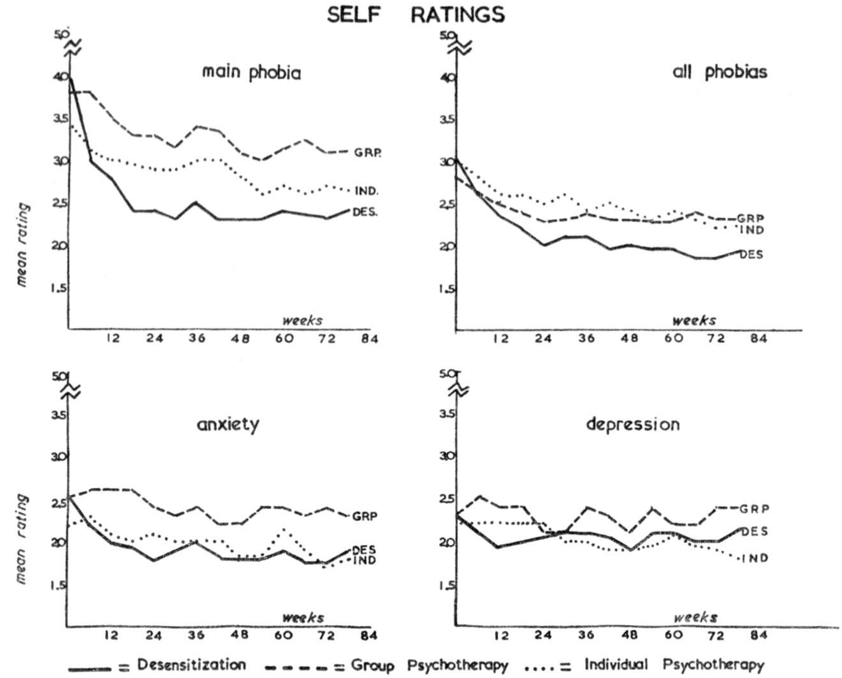

FIGURE 11. Mean self-ratings of four symptoms by patients receiving desensitization, individual psychotherapy and group psychotherapy. Reproduced from Gelder, Marks and Wolff (1967).

Finally, some of the authors' concluding comments are slightly puzzling. For example, they say that the results suggest "that psychotherapy need not be given routinely to all patients after successful desensitization" (p. 70). Why one should consider using a demonstrably inferior method (psychotherapy) is by no means clear — why one should consider using a demonstrably inferior method after successful treatment by desensitization is a riddle. Nevertheless, Marks and Gelder's investigations are the best field trials available, and need to be studied carefully by all students of behavior therapy.

The report made by Meyer and Crisp (1966) is particularly interesting, because they describe their experiences with the use of behavior therapy in a general psychiatric department which offers a wide range of diagnostic and treatment services, and which caters for a heterogeneous group of patients. They quote the results obtained with fifty-four cases of mixed neurotic and behavior disorders ranging from agoraphobia to encopresis. A variety of behavioral methods was used, and desensitization was the most common: The overall improvement rate was 70 per cent in a mean of twenty-five sessions. Only two relapses were noted and both of these were successfully re-treated.

Hain, Butcher and Stevenson (1966) presented a similar report of the clinical experiences except that they used only desensitization therapy. The work was, however, done in a general psychiatric department which resembles that in which the Meyer and Crisp study was conducted. All of the twenty-seven patients treated by Hain and his colleagues were diagnosed as suffering from psychoneuroses, and the duration of their symptoms ranged from four months to fifty years, with a mean of 8.6 years. The major symptoms encountered in these patients were fears and anxiety, and phobias. Seventy-eight per cent of the patients showed symptomatic improvement and 70 per cent showed marked general improvement. These figures are of course strikingly similar to those reported by Meyer and Crisp.

The mean number of sessions required to treat patients was nineteen; this figure is also similar to Meyer and Crisp's experience. Hain *et al.* found there was no correlation between the degree of improvement obtained and the duration of treatment. The greatest improvement (in addition to the removal of the presenting symptom) was found in occupational functioning. Once again, although it was sought, no evidence of symptom substitution was elicited. Like Meyer and Crisp, these authors make some interesting comments about the practical difficulties encountered in the routine use of behavior therapy (e.g., the selection of patients, the assessment of improvement, and so on).

Naturally, it is not sufficient merely to state that behavior therapy can successfully induce improvement in neurotic conditions, particularly anxiety states. Ideally one would like to know what the effective act in these types of treatment is. It has already been argued in the previous chapter that a number of the variables involved in desensitization therapy are not capable of inducing these improvements in isolation. For example, there is clear evidence that sheer muscle relaxation cannot by itself produce therapeutic improvements. Similarly, the improvements cannot be attributed to suggestibility, nor to hypnosis.

A more serious possibility is the one which was raised by Cooper (1963), Meyer and Gelder (1963), and by Murray (1962), among others. Pointing to the measure of success which can be obtained by other forms of treatment, it has been argued that the primary cause of the therapeutic improvements must be attributed to the patient-therapist relationship which develops during the course of treatment. However, if this were the main vehicle of change, then it would be difficult to account for the fact that in most studies behavior therapy appears to be more effective than other types of treatment. Fortunately we have some direct and indirect evidence which puts us in a position to estimate the contribution made to the progress of the therapy by the relationship between the patient and the therapist.

It should be pointed out initially that the contribution made by the relationship almost certainly varies with the type of disorder under consideration. In some types of disorder, particularly those which are complex and long lasting, the relationship seems to be of some significance. Examples of this type are provided by Meyer and Gelder (1963). In other disorders, however, such as enuresis, the relationship is of virtually no significance in determining the outcome of behavioral treatment.

Costello (1965) has drawn attention to an important difference between conventional types of psychotherapy and behavior therapy. He points out that many psychotherapists actively encourage the patient to form a close and even dependent emotional relationship with the therapist. In behavior therapy, this type of emotional bond is discouraged, as it is considered to be a possible source of interference with the relearning process.

Obviously the behavior therapist requires the cooperation of his patients and at all times avoids giving them cause for distrust or distress. It must also be recognized that the therapist is a potential and powerful source of social reinforcement (see

Ferster, 1958). The therapist can also facilitate the reduction of anxiety in a formal manner (by relaxation, etc.), or in an informal manner by verbal conditioning and reassurance. In the treatment of children he can reduce anxiety by directly comforting the patient (Bentler, 1963).

Commenting on this problem, Eysenck and Rachman (1965) say that "it is preferable, and indeed necessary, to analyse the effect of the relationship in learning-theory terms rather than in psychoanalytic or psychodynamic manner. Explanations which rely on the concepts of psychosexuality and/or unconscious motives and ideas cannot accommodate some of the available evidence. In particular, the results obtained in the treatment of enuresis defy explanation in dynamic terms. Similarly, it is impossible to speak of a transference or counter-transference effect in attempting to account for the successful reduction of neurotic disturbances in animals by means of direct comforting and soothing (see the work of Anderson and Parmenter, 1941; Masserman, 1943; Haslerud *et al.,* 1954; for examples)."

One might also add the recently accumulated evidence on the experimental use of systematic desensitization treatment for excessive fears in normal subjects. In many of these studies the extent and degree of the interaction between the therapist and the subject was minimal. Nevertheless, significant reductions in fear were regularly obtained. Moreover, in some studies, such as that reported by Lang, Lazovik and Reynolds (1965), even though a positive relationship was formed between the therapist and the subject, very little therapeutic change was produced except when systematic desensitization was conducted.

In the pseudo-therapy group used by these workers, the subjects reported that they had in fact developed a positive relationship. However, their fear of snakes was not significantly reduced despite the growth of such a relationship. It should be mentioned, however, that Paul (1965) obtained some evidence of beneficial effects emerging from the development of a relationship between the therapist and the subject. He noted that some subjects showed a measure of improvement which can apparently be attributed to their positive feelings regarding the pseudotherapists.

It seems reasonable to conclude that "the chief therapeutic contribution is made by the *deliberate and systematic* inhibition or extinction of the neurotic habit patterns — by deliberately facilitating the learning process" (Eysenck and Rachman, 1965).

Direct evidence in support of this conclusion can be found in the number of case reports. Wolpe (1962) described in great detail the treatment of a patient suffering from travel phobias and demonstrated very clearly the close correspondence between the stages completed in the desensitization of the travel hierarchy and the actual changes in the behavior of the patient outside the consulting room.

Along similar lines, Clark (1963) successfully treated a patient who suffered from a monosymptomatic phobia of birds and feathers. During the treatment he recorded her GSR changes and observed a progressive increase in basal skin resistance (and decreased GSR's) which corresponded closely with her progress up the desensitization hierarchy. The argument that relearning is the effective act is further supported by the fact that in Wolpe's travel-phobic patient, the woman's behavioral improvement continued to keep pace with her progress in the desensitization sessions even when the therapist was changed.

If the effective mechanism in behavior therapy is conceived of as being a relearning process, then it should be possible to manipulate and measure the techniques in a similar manner to the familiar learning processes. In 1963, Wolpe attempted the exercise by quantifying the relationships between the amount of training (learning trials) and the development of the learned reaction; he was able to demonstrate some interesting differences between what he called *proximation phobias* and other phobias.

He found, for example, that "in claustrophobias and phobias in which anxiety arises with increasing proximity to a feared object," only a small number of practice trials (i.e., desensitization presentations of the scene) were required to reduce the anxiety experienced at a far distance from the feared object. As the feared object is approached, however, an increasing number of practice trials is required. This positively accelerating curve is a familiar feature of many learning processes.

The relationships adduced by Wolpe are illustrated in the two figures below. In the first figure it can be seen how various proximation phobias take the same course of development; that an increasing number of scene presentations is required as one approaches the feared object itself. In the second diagram three cases of claustrophobia are described — once again it can be seen that the number of presentations required to eliminate the phobic reactions increases as the nucleus of the phobia is approached.

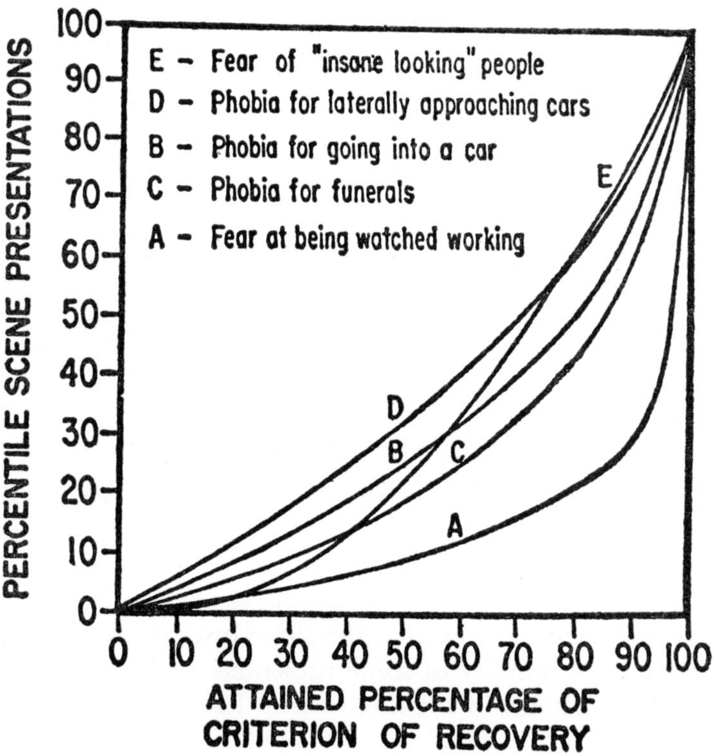

FIGURE 12. Response to desensitization treatment in proximation phobias. Reproduced from Wolpe (1963) (*Amer. J. Psychiat.*).

In the case of agoraphobias and other phobias which increase in intensity with the number of objects involved, the initial items on the hierarchy may be difficult to overcome (i.e., may require many practice trials). In this case the learning curve corresponds

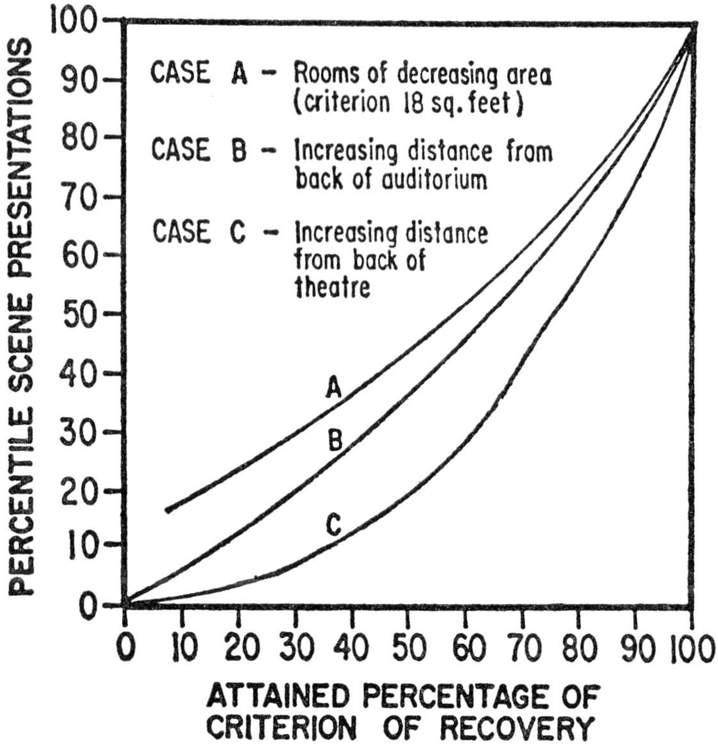

FIGURE 13. Response to desensitization treatment in claustrophobia. Reproduced from Wolpe (1963 (*Amer. J. Psychiat.*).

to a negatively accelerating function as illustrated in Figure 14 below. Here it can be seen that the three cases treated by Wolpe required a large number of scene presentations in order to cope with the initial items in the hierarchical list.

Translated into actual clinical practice this means that agoraphobics, for example, require a great deal of desensitization treatment before they can be helped to make the initial break out of their encapsulated circles. Once they have succeeded in moving beyond the restriction imposed by their phobic reactions, their progress tends to be fairly rapid and can ordinarily be achieved with considerably less effort than that which has gone into the initial attempts to get the person moving again.

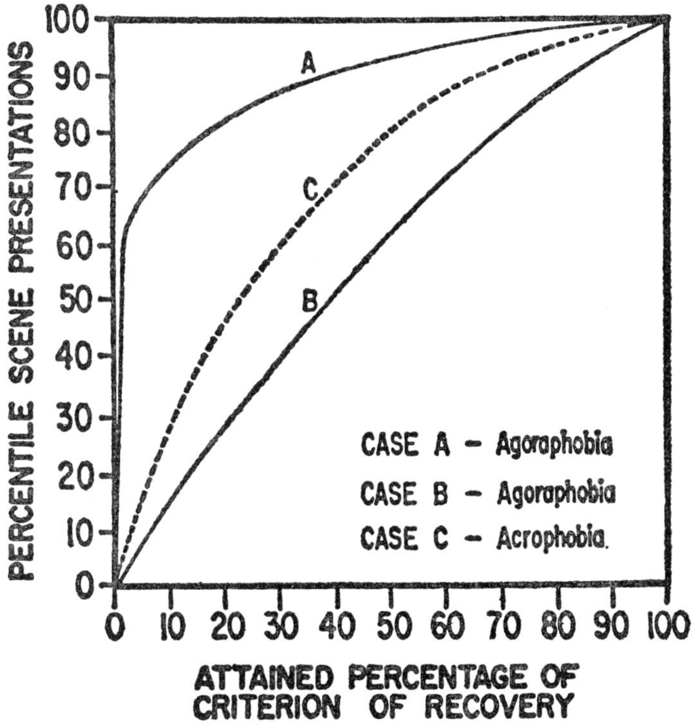

FIGURE 14. Response to desensitization treatment in agoraphobia and acrophobia. Reproduced from Wolpe (1963) (*Amer. J. Psychiat.*).

Apart from their relevance to the consideration of isolating the effective mechanisms in behavior therapy, these quantitative findings of Wolpe's show how therapeutic actions and reactions can be measured. Furthermore, they indicate how the lawful progression of the therapeutic learning process can be brought under close examination. The accumulation of further quantified observations of this type is highly desirable, and it is to be hoped that eventually one may be in the position to make reasonably accurate prognoses for the various types of phobias. It should also be possible to make reasonably accurate predictions about the expected speed of progression from session to session with different types of disorders and different types of patients.

The evidence to date on the effectiveness of behavior therapy has been summarized by Rachman (1965) in this way: "It is a promising technique which is virtually certain to be effective in a large number of phobic and anxiety states, but the treatment of severe chronic patients needs to be improved. There is, of course, a great need of further prospective controlled trials of the methods of behaviour therapy."

On the theoretical side, some important advances should be noted. When behavior therapy was first introduced, numerous objections were raised. Two of the most serious and widely expressed criticisms were these: On one hand it was argued that the tendency of behavior therapists to treat the observable manifestations of neurotic behavior would, if successful, lead to symptom substitution. That is to say, the patient would develop new and possibly worse symptoms if the so-called defensive reactions were removed. This phenomenon of symptom substitution has proved to be of minimum importance and occurs rarely (see Ch. V). There are more than a dozen studies in which symptom substitution was sought and in no instance was it found to be a serious problem, or indeed a common one. The experiments of Lang and Lazovik and the retrospective analysis carried out by Marks and others are good examples of this type of investigation (see Rachman, 1959, for further discussion of this point).

A second objection raised was that it is impossible to bring about a reduction or elimination of phobic and other neurotic symptoms and behavior unless one eliminates the presumed basic causes of the illness. It was said that behavior therapy could not succeed because it was directing its attention to the wrong quarters. This objection, too, has been eliminated (see Ch. V). In the experimental investigations and clinical reports there is clear evidence that substantial improvements in phobic and other neurotic behavior can be obtained by behavior therapy even when little or no attention is paid to the possible or presumed causes of the illness. The elimination of these two objections is, of course, an important step forward.

We now appear to have reached the point when the theoretical arguments for and against behavior therapy must be put to the test of careful clinical trials. There is, as we have shown, considerable evidence which supports the early claims made by Wolpe (1958), Eysenck (1964), and others that behavior therapy can be molded into a highly effective form of treatment for the neuroses. The controlled trials which have been planned or are at present under way will, it is hoped, indicate more clearly the range of application and the degree of success which can be obtained with these new methods of treatment based on learning procedures.

It is also important to bear in mind that the theory underlying the techniques of behavior therapy has wider value as an attempt to account for neurotic behavior and its manifestations (e.g., spontaneous remissions, relapses, and so on). The general account of neurotic behavior elaborated in this theory merits attention in its own right (see Eysenck and Rachman, 1965).

The evidence provided by the clinical reports described here is suggestive, but not firmly conclusive. A definitive decision must await further controlled studies in which the selection procedures, methods of assessment, follow-up investigations and other aspects of the therapy must be examined. However, these clinical reports, starting with Wolpe's original account, contribute to the development of a scientifically based therapy in two ways.

First, they lead to refinements of the techniques which are used in treating neurotic patients; and second, they enable one to construct hypotheses on which to base further investigations.

Two hypotheses which arise out of this information may be stated as follows. First, phobic (and other neurotic) patients treated by means of therapeutic procedures based on learning theory improve significantly more quickly than do patients treated by other types of therapy or who are not treated at all. Second, behavior therapy is able to achieve a higher rate of recovery than other types of therapy or no therapy at all.

Chapter VII

THE TREATMENT OF PHOBIAS: ADDITIONAL TECHNIQUES

MODIFICATIONS OF THE DESENSITIZATION TECHNIQUE

THE USE OF DRUGS to facilitate or supplement the desensitization treatment procedure has received surprisingly little attention. A recent modification of the treatment described by Friedman (1966a, 1966b) is therefore of particular interest. In this method the patient is relaxed by the injection of methohexitone sodium (Brietal®) and then desensitized. After the completion of the psychiatric history and the construction of the anxiety hierarchies, the patient is given an intravenous injection to induce a feeling of calm and relaxation.

The preparation is a 2.5 per cent solution, prepared by adding 20 ml distilled water to 500 mg methohexitone sodium. The administration of the drug is continued in order to maintain the patient in a state of calmness and relaxation, and the needle is kept in the vein throughout the treatment session. "The quantity of Brietal used is only sufficient to induce the required degree of relaxation without impairment of intellectual capacity, ..." (Friedman, 1966a). According to this account, approximately 25 to 50 mg is commonly necessary, and the amount of the drug used from session to session remains almost constant for each patient.

Although recovery from the drug is said to take place fairly rapidly and there is no amnesia for the interview, the possible side effects and after effects will need to be examined very carefully. Friedman reports successful results with all twenty-five consecutive cases of phobic anxiety seen in the Out-Patient's Department at St. Bartholomew's Hospital. This remarkable result has of course aroused considerable interest, and the technique is now being examined by a number of research workers.

The apparent advantages offered by this chemical technique are that it is capable of inducing rapid and deep relaxation without impairing the patient's ability to imagine the anxiety-evoking stimuli. It is possible in this way to eliminate not only the preliminary training in relaxation, but also to reduce the duration of each treatment session. Moreover, it enables treatment to be offered to even those patients who experience difficulty in acquiring skill in relaxation.

The replication and extension of Friedman's technique appears to be a worthwhile undertaking. Obviously such examination should make due allowance for the possible effects of the drug as such, and it would be necessary to provide controls for the effect of the Brietal acting independently of the desensitization procedure.

Some preliminary results from a study of this nature carried out by Drs. Sergeant and Yorkston and the author give grounds for encouragement. Twelve agoraphobic patients were treated in a study which employed an incomplete block design with each subject acting as his own control. A comparison was made between four different techniques; Brietal desensitization, Brietal alone, desensitization under relaxation, desensitization with the administration of a placebo injection. The preliminary indications from this as-yet-unpublished report are that the Brietal desensitization technique may prove to be an accelerated method of treating agoraphobia.* Naturally, further investigations will be required before it is possible to reach a definite conclusion on this method, and the long-term effectiveness of the technique will need to be demonstrated.

Two brief case histories will illustrate this method and its effectiveness.

> Friedman (1966b) described the successful treatment of a sixty-six-year-old deaf mute who complained of an intense phobia of dogs. The phobia had developed eight months previously and had serious repercussions on his day-to-day activities, including an inability to get to work because of the fear of encountering a dog. The phobia started after the patient had been attacked by an Alsatian dog on his way home from work. Because it was impossible to use verbal methods to treat this patient, a series of pictures of dogs was arranged in ascend-

*Unfortunately these indications were not borne out in the final analysis (to be published).

ing order of size and ferocity and then presented to the patient in gradual sequence while he was under the relaxing influence of an intravenous injection of Brietal. "The nonanxiety induced by the methohexitone sodium reciprocally inhibited the anxiety evoked by the pictures. After six sessions the patient was able to look calmly at a colored photograph of an Alsatian dog jumping up at a small boy. At the subsequent visit his daughter stated that her father was now a "different man." His anxiety concerning dogs was completely gone. This patient was followed up and after a period of six months was still symptom free."

A second methodological innovation which merits clinical investigation is the administration of *group desensitization.* The experiments of Lazarus (1961, 1966), Paul and Shannon (1966), Kondas (1967), and the author's experience of group treatment suggest that it may prove to be as effective as individual treatment. Paul and Shannon even go so far as to suggest that it might prove to be slightly superior to individual treatment; this may, however, simply reflect the type of problem concerned in their study: social anxiety.

Some indication of the clinical effectiveness of group desensitization was provided by Bannister and is referred to in Eysenck and Rachman (1965). Pending clinical confirmation of the efficacy of group desensitization treatment, it can be recommended as an economic alternative to individual procedures. It is to be expected, however, that some patients will not progress particularly well in group sessions (primarily because their anxiety hierarchies may be atypical) and that such patients will still require individual treatment. Some indication of the interfering effects of disparities between the hierarchies of different subjects in the same treatment group is given by Kondas (1967).

A third adaptation of the desensitization procedure is being explored by Lang (1966) and his colleagues. Following on their extremely important experimental studies, these psychologists have been attempting to automate the desensitization technique. In practice this means that the relaxation instructions and the anxiety hierarchies are presented to the patients on tape recordings and by other automatic devices. The early indications are that this automated form of treatment may be as effective (or even more effective!) than the normal desensitization procedure.

Apart from its interest as a practical proposition, the automatic execution of desensitization treatment is of very considerable theoretical interest. If it can be shown that the procedure is indeed effective, then it will provide strong evidence in support of the view that the development and maintenance of a patient-therapist relationship is of minor significance in determining the successful reduction or elimination of phobic (and other?) neurotic disorders.

Independent support for the early results mentioned by Lang and his coworkers is provided in the case history described by Migler and Wolpe (1967). They described the successful treatment of a patient who complained of a fear of public-speaking by means of "remote control" treatment.

> The patient was given seven treatment sessions administered by tape recordings which the patient played to himself. These recordings included instructions for relaxation and the presentation of the relevant hierarchy items which were recorded in ascending order. The patient was required to manipulate the recordings in such a way as to avoid the arousal of excessive anxiety, and he was apparently successful in monitoring his own treatment. He was followed up for four months and had maintained his successful response to treatment.

ASSERTIVE TRAINING

"A response which is antagonistic to anxiety and which can be easily invoked in social situations is self-assertion" (Eysenck and Rachman, 1965). The technique of *assertive training,* or *expressive training,* as it is sometimes called, was developed by Salter (1950). Although the theoretical notions underlying Salter's development of this procedure are of doubtful validity (he conceives of virtually all neurotic disorders as being problems of excessive inhibition), he has nevertheless succeeded in treating a wide range of neurotic disorders by this method. Although convincing experimental and clinical support for this technique is not yet available, it is, on the basis of clinical impressions reported by a number of psychologists and psychiatrists, a very useful procedure to use in treating social anxiety. Patients suffering from interpersonal anxiety (i.e., unadaptive emotional reactions which are evoked by the behavior, attitudes or appearance of other people) quite often respond well and fairly rapidly to this procedure.

The most likely explanation for the apparent success of assertive training in overcoming social anxiety is that the expression of emotional feelings of a positive kind reciprocally inhibits the anxiety which the patient normally experiences in the fear-provoking situation. The repeated inhibition of social anxiety by assertive behavior will result in the growth of a "negative habit," or more accurately, a conditioned inhibition of the social anxiety. More detailed descriptions of the assertive training procedure are provided by Salter (1950) Eysenck and Rachman (1965) and by Wolpe and Lazarus (1966).

In brief, the patient is encouraged to express his spontaneously felt emotions in a clear and forthright manner. He is also encouraged to express his emotions with free use of facial expression and is taught to express genuine differences of opinion with other people rather than to simulate agreement. He is encouraged to use the word I as much as possible. He is taught how to accept and express praise and to improvise and act spontaneously.

Stated in this brief manner, Salter's method of assertive training sounds reminiscent of the "pull yourself together" type of popular, platitudinous psychology. This can be quite misleading, however, as in practice these techniques are frequently of great effectiveness, judged solely on clinical impressions. Clearly a careful examination of the mode of action and the effectiveness of these procedures is essential.

A closely related technique is one which Wolpe and Lazarus describe as "behaviour rehearsal." This consists of assertive training combined with real-life rehearsals of anticipated social situations which are expected to give rise to anxiety. The patient and the therapist exchange roles in practice situations (e.g., interviews) until the patient is capable of behaving appropriately and without anxiety. It should be remembered, however, that Salter's methods of assertive training are most commonly used in combination with other behavior therapy techniques, notably systematic desensitization. Assertive training appears at this stage to be most appropriate in handling interpersonal (social) fears and anxiety.

THE USE OF SEXUAL RESPONSES

In systematic desensitization treatment, relaxation is used as a vehicle for counterconditioning the patient's anxiety. Small amounts of anxiety are deliberately provoked and then inhibited by the relaxation which the therapist induces in the patient. The repeated superimposition of the antagonistic relaxation response upon anxiety reactions produces a cumulative inhibitory effect which eventually terminates and eliminates the unwanted, unadaptive response pattern.

Sexual responses are, like relaxation, incompatible with anxiety reactions and have therefore been used on occasions as the counterconditioning mechanism. Gantt (1949) points out that ". . . sexual excitation has an inhibitory effect on the symptoms of anxiety." An account of the evidence supporting this observation is provided by Eysenck and Rachman (1965), who also describe the use of positive sexual responses in treating various types of sexual disorder.

The deliberate use of positive sexual excitation naturally finds its widest application in the treatment of fears associated with sexual situations. There are strong indications that this technique will prove to be of particular value in overcoming impotence and other types of sexual inadequacy. It is quite common to combine the use of positive sexual reactions with other treatment techniques, but most notably, desensitization and assertive training.

In their review, Eysenck and Rachman mention the handful of cases whose successful treatment had been described in the literature up to that time. The mean number of sessions required to bring about substantial improvements in five of the apparently cured cases of impotence was 14.4. These five patients were drawn from a series of seven reported by Wolpe (1958), and he noted that the two patients who suffered from interpersonal anxiety as well as impotence were decidedly more difficult to treat – seventy-five sessions were required in these cases. More recently, Wolpe and Lazarus (1966) have given an account of the results which they have obtained in treating thirty-one impotent patients. Of these, twenty-one (67.7%) were very much improved or completely recovered at the end of treatment. An additional six patients (19.4%) obtained limited but significant improvements. The mean age of the patients was thirty-six years and the mean time taken to obtain these results was 11.5 weeks.

The use of sexual responses as a means of overcoming fear is essentially simple. The concept of reciprocal inhibition treatment is explained to the patient and it is emphasized that positive sexual responses are a strong inhibitor of unadaptive anxiety. The patient is then given specific instructions about how to make proper use of positive sexual excitation. He is told to refrain from attempting any form of sexual activity unless he has an unmistakeable, positive desire to do so; he is also told to engage in graded and gradual sexual activity when the positive desire is present and when circumstances are propitious.

In the early stages of treatment the patient is strongly advised not to attempt intercourse until he feels strongly impelled to do so. Instead, he is asked gradually to approach full intercourse only after he has successfully engaged in relaxed sexual foreplay during which no anxiety should have been present. The patient is warned to terminate any sexual activity immediately if he detects the arousal of anxiety. Having been trained in relaxation, the patient is advised to induce relaxation by himself if and when anxiety arises in a sexual situation.

As positive sexual activity is ordinarily self-reinforcing, it is usual for these patients to obtain increasing satisfaction with successive experiences, provided they adhere to the instructions given to them by the therapist and avoid the risk of ever allowing a significant amount of anxiety to develop. The principle and practice underlying the use of sexual responses in the treatment of impotence can with slight modifications be used in helping to overcome problems of frigidity in women. There are a small number of reports of the successful treatment of this condition (Eysenck and Rachman, 1965; Rachman, 1963).

THE ANXIETY-RELIEF METHOD

"If an unpleasant stimulus is endured for several seconds and is then made to cease almost immediately after a specified signal, that signal may become conditioned to the changes that follow cessation of the uncomfortable stimulus. The patient experiences these changes as a feeling of relief" (Wolpe and Lazarus, 1966). In practice the unpleasant stimulus is an electric shock and the relief (which is produced by the termination of the shock) is associated with the word *Calm*. The patient is trained to "switch off" the discomfort caused by the electric shock merely by saying the word *Calm*.

Once a powerful association between anxiety-relief and the signal word has been established, the utterance of the word can in some cases induce a feeling of relaxation fairly rapidly. The patient is then able to control anxiety if and when it arises in disturbing situations. This procedure has not been used extensively, and at this stage it is difficult to make any confident predictions about its validity or efficacy.

A similar technique was developed by Thorpe *et al.* (1964) under the name of *Aversion-Relief*. Here again the aim was to condition an association between relief from unpleasant stimulation and a verbal (or other) cue. Thorpe and his colleagues obtained some interesting improvements with this procedure. Like that developed by Wolpe, the Aversion-Relief method needs considerable investigation before one can recommend its routine use.

THE TREATMENT OF FEAR IN CHILDREN

In her classic studies, Jones (1924, 1925) gave an account of several possible methods of treatment. They are direct conditioning, social imitation, systematic distraction, feeding responses, and affectional responses.

Feeding responses, like relaxation or sexual excitation, are incompatible with anxiety and can therefore be used as a means of inducing inhibition. Feeding was one of the inhibiting agents used by Jones in her famous case of Peter, the child with a rabbit phobia. The phobic-producing animal was gradually introduced into the room while Peter was eating his meal. By a series of careful steps the animal was brought into close proximity with the child while he continued to eat, and eventually he was able to tolerate the animal right next to him during the feeding period.

More recently, Lazarus (1961) published an account of the successful treatment of a phobic child with the use of feeding responses. As we now know, predominantly from experimental investigations of animals and also from clinical observation, the use of feeding responses must be carefully controlled if one is to avert the danger of producing an inhibition of eating instead of reducing the anxiety. This paradoxical effect can be produced if the process of approximation is accelerated unduly or if attempts are made to expose the child to the phobic situation when he is not willing or ready to eat. In other words, the treatment program involving the slow and gradual exposure of the child to the phobic situation should be undertaken only after a specified but limited period of deprivation. Carrying out the treatment during the child's customary mealtime is probably the safest way of proceeding, and it is important to ensure that the food which is to be used during the retraining session is desired and appetizing.

One of the most common techniques used by parents to relax or comfort their children is affectionate handling. The clinical use of affectional responses has to date been neglected. An illustration of its possible effectiveness is, however, given in a case reported by Bentler (1963) who described the successful treatment of an infant with a bath phobia by using affection as a direct inhibitor of anxiety.

Another technique for inhibiting anxiety and overcoming children's fears was developed by Lazarus and Abramovitz (1964), and is referred to by them as "the use of emotive imagery." This procedure is a variant on Wolpe's systematic desensitization technique and involves the substitution of imaginal evocations of parasympathetic emotions other than relaxation. In this method, it is unnecessary to provide a full course of relaxation training for the child before commencing desensitization. Instead, the child is trained to obtain vivid images of people or situations which produce positive emotions such as joy, mirth, pride, etc. The case reports described by the authors are convincing and encouraging, but like most of the techniques described in this chapter, the use of emotive imagery needs to be investigated more thoroughly before it can be recommended for routine use.

One of the most interesting of the recent developments in this field has been the reappearance of the technique of social imitation. It will be recalled that Jones obtained some successful results with this procedure in 1924. Following up his use of the concept of imitation to account for various aspects of child behavior, including the arousal of fear, Bandura has now made a systematic attempt to apply imitation as a clinical procedure. Bandura, Grusec and Menlove (1966) recently described the results of an experiment involving forty-eight nursery-school children ranging in age from three to five years. The children were assigned to one of four matched groups on the basis of parental ratings of their fearful behavior towards dogs. The children were also given a test of avoidance in the presence of a live dog.

The treatments given to the four groups of children were as follows. Each group consisted of four children who received 8 ten-minute treatment sessions on four consecutive days. The first group participated in a "modelling positive-context condition" in which they observed a fearless peer model display approach responses towards a dog within the context of an enjoyable party atmosphere. On successive treatment sessions the peer model made increasingly direct approaches to the animal. This form of imitation training proved to be successful and produced a significant reduction in the childrens' fear and avoidance behavior in the presence of a live dog after the completion of treatment. The reduction in fear was found, at a follow-up retest, to be stable. The children assigned to the second group received a "modelling neutral-context condition." In this procedure the children observed the same sequence of approach responses performed by the same peer model, but this time the party was omitted.

In each of the sessions the subjects were seated at a table and required to observe the performance of the fearless child. This imitative, therapeutic procedure also succeeded in reducing the dog phobias of the children concerned. As with the first group, these reductions in fear were found to be stable. The third group of children constituted a control group in order to exclude the possibility that the fear reductions obtained in the first two groups had been caused by the simple repetition of exposure to a positive party atmosphere and/or to the dog.

This treatment conditioning is called the *exposure positive-context condition* and it produced comparatively little improvement. The fourth group received "positive-context" training. "Here the children were never exposed to the dog but merely participated in the parties, and the main purpose of including this procedure was to determine whether the mere presence of a dog had an adverse or a beneficial effect on the children." This control group also showd no significant improvement.

In order to determine the generality of the improvements which had been obtained, half the children in each of the four groups were exposed to an unfamiliar animal at the termination of the treatment. The remaining children were presented with the experimental animal first and then an unfamiliar dog. The results of this variation indicated that the reduction in fear consequent upon the treatment "by imitation" generalized from the specific phobic object to related objects. Bandura *et al.* (1966) sum up the findings of the experiment in this way:

> They . . . provide considerable evidence that avoidance responses can be successfully extinguished on a vicarious basis. This is shown in the fact that children who experience a gradual exposure to progressively more fearful modelled responses displayed extensive and stable reductions in avoidance behaviour. Moreover, most of the subjects were able to engage in extremely intimate and potentially fearful interactions with test animals following the treatment series.

It is possible that treatment by social imitation will prove to be too cumbersome for use as a routine clinical procedure for overcoming children's phobias. Nevertheless, there are a number of situations in which it may prove to be of considerable value. Perhaps its greatest potential lies in the field of prevention rather than therapy. One possible application, for example, would be the systematic use of social imitation as a means of preventing the development of phobias regarding dental treatment. Another context in which social imitation may prove to be extremely valuable is in nursery and infant schools. There is a good deal of evidence to suggest that many children have anxiety reactions during the early period of their attendance at a new school (e.g., Slater, 1939) and the deliberate use of well-adapted and fearless children as models for new and possibly fearful pupils may well be worth developing.

RECAPITULATION

It should be evident from the range of additional techniques described here that there is a reasonable selection of therapeutic approaches which can be resorted to if the better-established technique of desensitization is inapplicable or ineffective. However, it should be noted that these supplementary techniques are without exception still in the early stages of development, and a considerable amount of experimental and clinical research will need to be done before they can be incorporated into the therapist's repertoire with any confidence. The alternative techniques described here are as follows: systematic desensitization conducted under drug-induced relaxation, group desensitization, automated desensitization, assertive training, the use of sexual responses, anxiety-relief techniques, the use of feeding responses, the use of affectional responses and the use of social imitation.

Appendix

THE GEER FEAR-SURVEY SCHEDULE II*

THE RATING SCALE consists of fifty-one items. Subjects are required to estimate their reactions on a seven point scale.

None	*Very little*	*A little*	*Some*	*Much*	*Very much*	*Terror*
1	2	3	4	5	6	7

The list of items and associated statistics follow.

Item	Mean Score		Item-Total Score Correlations	
	Men	*Women*	*Men*	*Women*
1. Sharp objects	1.60	1.87	.477	.434
2. Being a passenger in a car	.60	.93	.411	.527
3. Dead bodies	1.70	1.98	.592	.400
4. Suffocating	2.05	2.04	.510	.476
5. Failing a test	3.30	3.32	.411	.380
6. Looking foolish	2.79	2.94	.467	.575
7. Being a passenger in an airplane	1.26	1.79	.513	.448
8. Worms	.27	1.32*	3.55	.402
9. Arguing with parents	1.27	1.37	.493	.287
10. Rats and mice	1.03	2.33*	.568	.316
11. Life after death	.86	1.22	.455	.426
12. Hypodermic needles	1.50	1.89	.607	.312
13. Being criticized	1.98	2.30	.612	.573
14. Meeting someone for the first time	1.30	1.52	.496	.493
15. Roller coasters	1.32	1.99	.332	.222
16. Being alone	0.70	1.23	.548	.489
17. Making mistakes	2.22	2.52	.492	.578
18. Being misunderstood	1.74	1.94	.468	.471
19. Death	1.96	2.39	.538	.659
20. Being in a fight	1.83*	1.78	.585	.481
21. Crowded places	.72*	.77	.424	.431
22. Blood	.77*	.84	.550	.306
23. Heights	1.76	1.73	.461	.368
24. Being a leader	1.02	1.45	.497	.557
25. Swimming alone	.96	1.43	.474	.395
26. Illness	1.25	1.86	.568	.426
27. Being with drunks	1.16	2.63	.518	.463
28. Illness or injury to loved ones	3.11	4.08*	.534	.627
29. Being self-conscious	2.18	2.41	.648	.537
30. Driving a car	.48	1.06	.558	.492
31. Meeting authority	1.27	1.66	.546	.514
32. Mental illness	1.29	1.97	.516	.519
33. Closed places	.78	1.16	.434	.477
34. Boating	.53	1.88	.555	.532
35. Spiders	1.20	2.19*	.466	.472
36. Thunderstorms	.45	1.03	.482	.428

*From J. H. Geer (1965): *Behaviour Research and Therapy.*

37. Not being a success	2.79	2.28	.442	.597
38. God	1.35	1.50	.382	.313
39. Snakes	1.97	3.05*	.482	.482
40. Cemeteries	.71	1.24	.549	.546
41. Speaking before a group	2.59	2.87	.487	.484
42. Seeing a fight	.68	1.79*	.510	.477
42. Death of a loved one	3.41	4.25	.562	.489
44. Dark places	.95	1.67	.576	.481
45. Strange dogs	1.50	1.75	.524	.456
46. Deep water	1.22	2.02	.515	.607
47. Being with a member of the opposite sex	.68*	.62	.481	.365
48. Stinging insects	1.80	2.38	.565	.495
49. Untimely or early death	1.89	2.66	.555	.654
50. Losing a job	1.95	2.02	.475	.566
51. Auto accidents	2.05	2.98	.565	.596

All correlations are statistically significant at $p < .01$ except number 15 for women which is significant $p < .05$.
*Sex difference significantly larger than expected $p < .01$.

BIBLIOGRAPHY

AGRAS, W. S. (1965): An investigation of the decrement of anxiety responses during systematic desensitization therapy. *Behav. Res. Ther., 2:*267.

ANDERSON, O. D., and PARMENTER, R. (1941): A long-term study of the experimental neurosis in the sheep and dog. *Psychosom. Med. Monogr., 6:* (3, 4).

BANDURA, A. (1965): Vicarious processes: A case of no-trial learning. In *Advances in Experimental Social Psychology.* (Berkowitz, L., Ed.) New York, Academic, Vol. II.

BANDURA, A.; GRUSEC, J. E., and MENLOVE, F. L. (1966): Vicarious extinction of avoidance behaviour. *J. Pers. Soc. Psychol.,* (In press).

BANDURA, A., and WALTERS, R. H. (1963): *Social Learning and Personality Development.* New York, Holt.

BENTLER, P. M. (1962): An infant's phobia treated with reciprocal inhibition therapy. *J. Child Psychol. Psychiat., 3:*185.

BRILL, A. A. (1949): *Basic Principles of Psychoanalysis.* New York, Doubleday.

BROADHURST, P. L. (1960): Abnormal animal behaviour. In *Handbook of Abnormal Psychology.* (Eysenck, H. J., Ed.) London, Pitmans.

BURNETT, A., and RYAN, E. (1963): The application of conditioning techniques in psychotherapy in a day-care treatment hospital. Unpublished Report.

CLARK, D. F. (1963): Treatment of a monosymptomatic phobia by systematic desensitization. *Behav. Res. Ther., 1:*89.

COOKE, G. (1966): The efficacy of two desensitization procedures: An analogue study. *Behav. Res. Ther., 4:*17.

COOPER, J. E. (1963): A study of behaviour therapy in thirty psychiatric patients. *Lancet, 1:*411.

COOPER, J. E.; GELDER, M. G., and MARKS, I. M. (1965): Results of behaviour therapy in seventy-seven psychiatric patients. *Brit. Med. J., 1:*1222.

COSTELLO, C. G. (1963): Behaviour therapy: Criticisms and confusions. *Behav. Res. Ther., 1:*159.

CURRAN, D., and PARTRIDGE, M. (1955): *Psychological Medicine.* Edinburgh and London, Livingstone.

DAVISON, G. (1965): The influence of systematic desensitization, relaxation and graded exposure to imaginal stimuli in the modification of phobic behaviour. Unpublished doctoral dissertation, Stanford University.

DIETHELM, O. (1955): *Treatment in Psychiatry.* Springfield, Thomas.

ERRARA, P., and COLEMAN, J. V. (1963): A long-term follow-up study of neurotic phobic patients in a psychiatric clinic. *J. Nerv. Ment. Dis., 136:* 267.

ERWIN, W. J. (1963) : Confinement in the production of human neuroses: The barber's-chair syndrome. *Behav. Res. Ther., 1:*175.

EYSENCK, H. J. (Ed.) (1960) : *Behaviour Therapy and the Neuroses.* Oxford, Pergamon.

EYSENCK, H. J. (1963) : Behaviour therapy, spontaneous remission and transference in neurotics. *Amer. J. Psychiat., 119:*867.

EYSENCK, H. J. (1963) : Behaviour therapy, extinction and relapse in neurosis. *Brit. J. Psychiat., 109:*12.

EYSENCK, H. J. (Ed.) (1964) : *Experiments in Behaviour Therapy.* Oxford, Pergamon.

EYSENCK, H. J. (1967) : *The Biological Basis of Personality.* Springfield, Thomas.

EYSENCK, H. J. (1967) : Spontaneous remission in neurosis. In *Critical Issues in Clinical Psychology.* (O. B. Dent, Ed.) (In press) .

EYSENCK, H. J., and RACHMAN, S. (1965) : *The Causes and Cures of Neurosis.* London, Routledge and Kegan, Paul; San Diego, R. Knapp.

FERSTER, C. B. (1958) : Reinforcement and punishment in the control of human behaviour by social agencies. *Psychiat. Res. Rep., 10:*101.

FRIEDMAN, D. (1966a) : A new technique for the systematic desensitization of phobic symptoms. *Behav. Res. Ther., 4:*139.

FRIEDMAN, D. (1966b) : Treatment of a case of dog phobia in a deaf mute by behaviour therapy. *Behav. Res. Ther., 4:*141.

GALE, D.; STRUMFELS, G., and GALE, E. (1966) : A comparison of reciprocal inhibition and experimental extinction in the psychotherapeutic process. *Behav. Res. Ther., 4:*149.

GANTT, W. H. (1944) : Experimental basis for neurotic behavior. *Psychosom. Med. Monogr.,* No. 3.

GANTT, W. H. (1949) : Psychosexuality in animals. *Psychosexual Development in Health and Disease.* New York, Grune.

GANTT, W. H.; NEWTON, J., and ROYER, F. (1962) : Development of experimental neurosis. *Proc. III World Congress Psychiat.,* Montreal.

GEER, J. (1965) : The development of a scale to measure fear. *Behav. Res. Ther., 3:*45.

GELDER, M.; MARKS, I., and WOLFF, H. (1967) : Desensitization and psychotherapy in the treatment of phobic states. *Brit. J. Psychiat., 113:*53.

GELLHORN, E. (1964) : Motion and emotion. *Psychol. Rev., 71.*

GRAY, J. (1964) : *Pavlov's Typology; Recent Theoretical and Experimental Developments from the Laboratory of B. M. Teplov.* Oxford, Pergamon.

GRINKER, R. R., and SPIEGEL, J. P. (1945) : *Men Under Stress.* London, Churchill.

GROSSBERG, J., and WILSON, H. (1965) : A correlational comparison of the Wolpe-Lang Fear-Survey Schedule and Taylor MAS. *Behav. Res. Ther., 3:*125.

HAGMAN, R. (1932) : A study of fears in children of preschool age. *J. Exp. Psychol., 1:*110.

HAIN, J.; BUTCHER, R., and STEVENSON, I. (1966) : Systematic desensitization therapy: An analysis of results in twenty-seven patients. *Brit. J. Psychiat., 112:*295.

HASLERUD, G.; BRADBARD, L., and JOHNSTONE, R. (1954) : Pure guidance and handling as components of the Maier technique for breaking fixations. *J. Psychol., 37:*27.

HENDERSON, D., and GILLESPIE, R. D. (1950) : *Textbook of Psychiatry for Students and Practitioners.* Oxford U. P.

HENDRICK, I. (1948) : *Facts and Theories of Psychoanalysis.* New York, Knopf.

HOLMES, F. (1935) : An experimental study of fears of young children. In *Children's Fears.* (Jersild, A., and Homes, F., Eds.) *Child Develp. Monogr.,* No. 20.

HUMPHERY, J. (1966) : Behaviour therapy with children: An experimental evaluation. *Ph.D. Thesis., Univ. of London.*

HUSSAIN, A. (1964) : Behaviour therapy using hypnosis. In *The Conditioning Therapies.* (Wolpe, Salter and Reyna, Eds.) New York, Holt.

JACOBSON, E. (1938) : *Progressive Relaxation.* Chicago, U. of Chicago.

JERSILD, A. T., and HOLMES, F. (1935) : Children's Fears. *Child Develpm. Monogr.,* No. 20.

JOHN, E. (1941) : A study of the effects of evacuation and air raids on preschool children. *Brit. J. Educ. Psychol., 11:*173.

JONES, M. C. (1924) : A laboratory study of fear: The case of Peter. *Pedagog. Sem., 31:*308.

KONDAS, O. (1967) : Reduction of examination anxiety and "stage-fright" by group desensitization and relaxation. *Behav. Res. Ther.,* (In press) .

KURTZ, K., and WALTERS, G. (1962) : The effects of prior experiences on an approach-avoidance conflict. *J. Comp. Physiol. Psychol., 55:*1075.

LADER, M. H. (1966) : Predictive value of autonomic measures in patients with phobic states. *D.P.M. Dissertation, Univ. of London.*

LADER, M. H., and WING, L. (1966) : *Physiological measures, sedative drugs, and morbid anxiety. Maudsley Monographs,* No. 14.

LANG, P. J. (1966) : Fear reduction and fear behaviour: problems in treating a construct. *3rd Conference on Research in Psychotherapy,* Chicago, June, 1966.

LANG, P., and LAZOVIK, A. (1963) : The experimental desensitization of a phobia. *J. Abnorm. Soc. Psychol., 66:*519.

LANG, P.; LAZOVIK, A., and REYNOLDS, D. (1966) : Desensitization, suggestibility and pseudotherapy. *J. Abnorm. Psychol., 70:*395.

LANYON, R., and MANOSEVITZ, M. (1967) : Validity of self-reported fear. *Behav. Res. Ther.,* (In press) .

LAPOUSE, R., and MONK, M. (1959) : Fears and worries in a representative sample of children. *Amer. J. Orthopsychiat., 29:*803.

LAZARUS, A. A. (1960): The elimination of children's phobias by deconditioning. In *Behaviour Therapy and the Neuroses.* (Eysenck, H. J., Ed.) Oxford, Pergamon.

LAZARUS, A. A. (1963): The results of behaviour therapy in 126 cases of severe neurosis. *Behav. Res. Ther., 1*:65.

LAZARUS, A. A. (1964): Crucial procedural factors in desensitization therapy. *Behav. Res. Ther., 2*:59.

LIDDELL, H. (1944): Conditioned reflex method and experimental neurosis. In *Personality and the Behaviour Disorders.* (Hunt, J. Mc.V., Ed.) New York, Ronald.

LOMONT, J. F. (1965): Reciprocal inhibition or extinction? *Behav. Res. Ther., 3*:209.

LOMONT, J. F., and EDWARDS, J. E. (1967): The role of relaxation in systematic desensitization. *Behav. Res. Ther., 5*:11.

MACFARLANE, J. M.; ALLEN, L., and HONZIK, M. (1954): *A Developmental Study of the Behavior Problems of Normal Children.* Berkeley, U. of Calif.

MARKS, I., and GELDER, M. (1965): A controlled retrospective study of behaviour therapy in phobic patients. *Brit. J. Psychiat., III*:561.

MARKS, I., and GELDER, M. (1966): Severe agoraphobia: A controlled prospective trial of behaviour therapy. *Brit. J. Psychiat., 112*:309.

MARKS, I. M., and GELDER, M. G. (1966): Different ages of onset in varieties of phobia. *Amer. J. Psychiat., 123*:218.

MASSERMAN, J. H. (1943): *Behaviour and Neurosis.* Chicago, U. of Chicago.

MASSERMAN, J. H. (1955): *The Practice of Dynamic Psychiatry.* New York, Saunders.

MAY, R. (1950): *The Meaning of Anxiety.* New York, Ronald.

MAYER-GROSS, W.; SALTER, E., and ROTH, A. (1960): *Clinical Psychiatry.* London, Cassell.

METZNER, R. (1961): Learning theory and the therapy of the neuroses. *Brit. J. Psychol. Monogr.,* Suppl. 33.

MEYER, V., and CRISP, A. H. (1966): Some problems of behaviour therapy. *Brit. J. Psychiat., 112*:367.

MEYER, V., and GELDER, M. G. (1963): Behaviour therapy and complex disorders. *Brit. J. Psychiat., 109*:19.

MIGLER, B., and WOLPE, J. (1967): Automated self-desensitization: A case report. *Behav. Res. Ther.,* (In press).

MILLER, N. (1951): Learnable drives and rewards. In *Handbook of Experimental Psychology.* (S. S. Stevens, Ed.) New York, Wiley.

MILLER, N. E. (1960): Learning resistance to pain and fear. *J. Exp. Psychol., 60*:137.

MOORE, N. (1965): Behaviour therapy in bronchial asthma: A controlled study. *J. Psychosom. Res., 9*:257.

MOWRER, O. H. (1939): Stimulus-response theory of anxiety. *Psychol. Rev., 46*:553.

MURRAY, E. J. (1962): Paper at A.P.A. Convention, St. Louis. Quoted by Costello, C. G. (1963).

NAPALKOV, A. V. (1963): Information process of the brain. *Progress in Brain Research.* (Wiener and Schade, Eds.) Amsterdam, Elsevier.

NOYES, A. P., and KOLB, L. C. (1958): *Modern Clinical Psychiatry.* London, Saunders.

PAUL, G. (1966): *Insight versus Desensitization in Psychotherapy.* Stanford, Stanford.

PAUL, G., and SHANNON, D. (1966): Treatment of anxiety through systematic desensitization in therapy groups. *J. Abnorm. Psychol., 71*:124.

PAVLOV, I. O. (1927): *Conditioned Reflexes.* London, Oxford U. P.

RACHMAN, S. (1958): Objective psychotherapy: Some theoretical considerations. *S. Afr. Med. J., 33*:19.

RACHMAN, S. (1961): Sexual disorders and behaviour therapy. *Amer. J. Psychiat., 118*:235.

RACHMAN, S. (1963): Inhibition and disinhibition in schizophrenics. *Arch. Gen. Psychiat., 8*:91.

RACHMAN, S. (1965): The current status of behaviour therapy. *Arch. Gen. Psychiat., 13*:418.

RACHMAN, S. (1965): Studies in desensitization: I. The separate effects of relaxation and desensitization. *Behav. Res. Ther., 3*:245.

RACHMAN, S. (1966a): Studies in desensitization: II: Flooding. *Behav. Res. Ther., 4*:1.

RACHMAN, S. (1966b): Studies in desensitization. III: Speed of generalization. *Behav. Res. Ther., 4*:7.

RACHMAN, S., and COSTELLO, C. G. (1961): The aetiology and treatment of childrens' phobias: A review. *Amer. J. Psychiat., 118*:97.

RAMSAY, R. W. *et al.* (1966): Massed versus spaced desensitization of fear. *Behav. Res. Ther., 4*:205.

RUBIN, B.; KATKIN, R., and WEISS, G. (1967): Factor-analysis of a fear survey schedule. (In preparation).

SALTER, A. (1950): *Conditioned Reflex Therapy.* New York, Creative Age Press.

SANDERSON, R. E.; CAMPBELL, D., and LAVERTY, S. G. (1962): Traumatically conditioned responses acquired during respiratory paralysis. *Nature, 196*:1235.

SCHMIDT, E.; CASTELL, D., and BROWN, P. (1965): A retrospective study of 42 cases of behaviour therapy. *Behav. Res. Ther., 3*:9.

SHIELDS, J. (1962): *Monozygotic Twins Brought Up Apart and Brought Up Together.* Oxford U. P.

SLATER, E. (1939): Responses to a nursery-school situation. *Soc. Res. Child Develop. Monogr.,* No. 4, Vol. II.

SLATER, S., and LEAVY, A. (1966): The effects of inhaling a 35 per cent CO_2 and 65 per cent O_2 mixture upon anxiety level in neurotic patients. *Behav. Res. Ther., 4*:309.

TEASDALE, J. (1966) : The efficacy of desensitization in subjects with high or low neuroticism. Unpublished research report, Inst. of Psychiatry, London.

THORPE, J.; SCHMIDT, E., and CASTELL, D. (1964) : A comparison of positive and negative (aversive) conditioning in the treatment of homosexuality. *Behav. Res. Ther., 1*:357.

ULLMANN, L., and KRASNER, L. (1965) : *Case Studies in Behaviour Modification.* New York, Holt.

WALTERS, G. C. (1963) : Frequency and intensity determinants of fearfulness. *Canad. J. Psychol., 17*:412.

WALK, R. D. (1956) : Self-ratings of fear in a fear-evoking situation. *J. Abnorm. Soc. Psychol., 52*:171.

WATSON, J. B., and RAYNER, R. (1920) : Conditioned emotional reactions. *J. Exp. Psychol., 3*:1.

WOLPE, J. (1958) : *Psychotherapy by Reciprocal Inhibition.* Stanford, Stanford Univ. Press.

WOLPE, J. (1961) : The systematic desensitization treatment of neuroses. *J. Nerv. Ment. Dis., 132*:189.

WOLPE, J. (1962) : Experimental foundations of some new psychotherapeutic methods. In *Experimental Foundations of Clinical Psychology.* (Bachrach, A. J., Ed.) New York, Basic Books.

WOLPE, J. (1963) : Behaviour therapy in complex neurotic states. *Brit. J. Psychiat., 110*:28.

WOLPE, J. (1963) : Quantitative relationships in the systematic desensitization of phobias. *Amer. J. Psychiat., 119*:1062.

WOLPE, J. (1964) : Personal communication.

WOLPE, J., and LANG, P. (1964) : A fear-survey schedule for use in behaviour therapy. *Behav. Res. Ther., 2*:27.

WOLPE, J., and LAZARUS, A. (1966) : *Behaviour Therapy Techniques.* Oxford, Pergamon.

WOLPE, J., and RACHMAN, S. (1960) : Psychoanalytic evidence: A critique based on Freud's case of Little Hans. In *Critical Essays on Psychoanalysis.* (Rachman, S., Ed.) Oxford, Pergamon.

WOLPE, J.; SALTER, A., and REYNA, J. (1964) : *The Conditioning Therapies: The Challenge in Psychotherapy.* New York, Holt.

WOODWARD, J. (1959) : Emotional disturbances of burned children. *Brit. Med. J., 1*:1009.

INDEX